# The Great Adventure by Arnold Bennett

Arnold Bennett was born in 1867 in Hanley, one of the six towns that formed the Potteries that later joined together to become Stoke-on-Trent - the area in which most of his works are located.

For a short time he worked for his solicitor father before realising that to advance his life he would need to become his own man. Moving to London at 21, he obtained work as a solicitor's clerk and gradually moved into a career of Journalism.

At the turn of the century he turned full time to writing and shortly thereafter, in 1903, he moved to Paris.

In 1908 Bennett published The Old Wives' Tale, to great acclaim. With this, his reputation was set. Clayhanger and The Old Wives' Tale are perhaps his greatest and most lauded novels. But standing next to these are many fine short stories. Bennett bathes us in vignettes of life, replete with characters that are easy to immerse ourselves in, whatever their ambitions may be.

Here we publish his play 'The Great Adventure'. As with anything written by Bennett it's a fabulous showcase for his literary talents.

## Table of Contents
Characters
Schedule of Scenes
Act 1 Scene 1
Act 1 Scene 2
Act 2 Scene 1
Act 2 Scene 2
Act 3 Scene 1
Act 3 Scene 2
Act 4 Scene 1
Act 4 Scene 2

## Characters
| | |
|---|---|
| ILAM CARVE | An illustrious Painter |
| ALBERT SHAWN | Ilam's Valet |
| DR. PASCOE | |
| EDWARD HORNING | Doctor's Assistant |
| CYRUS CARVE | Ilam's Cousin, a City Auctioneer |
| FATHER LOOE | A Catholic Priest |
| PETER HORNING | A Journalist |
| EBAG | A Picture Dealer |
| JOHN SHAWN | A Curate |
| JAMES SHAWN | His Brother, a Curate |
| LORD LEONARD ALCAR | |
| TEXEL | An American Millionaire |
| A WAITER | |
| A PAGE | |
| A SERVANT | |

JANET CANNOT         A Widow
MRS. ALBERT SHAWN
HONORIA LOOE       Sister of Father Looe

## SCENES

ACT I - ROOM IN ILAM CARVE'S HOUSE, 126 REDCLIFFE GARDENS

ACT II - PRIVATE ROOM AT THE GRAND BABYLON HOTEL

ACT III - JANET'S SITTING-ROOM AT WERTER ROAD, PUTNEY

ACT IV - LORD LEONARD ALCAR'S STUDY, GROSVENOR GARDENS

SPECIAL NOTE. Each Act is divided into two scenes, separated by a passage of time more or less short. The passage of time is indicated by darkening the stage for a few moments. No change of scenery is involved.

NOTE

The play was produced for the first time in London at the Kingsway Theatre, by Granville Barker, on Tuesday, March 25th, 1913.

THE GREAT ADVENTURE

### ACT I SCENE I
[Front room on ground floor at 126 Redcliffe Gardens. An apartment furnished richly but in an old-fashioned way. Fine pictures. Large furniture. Sofa near centre. General air of neglect and dustiness. Carpet half-laid. Trunks and bags lying about in corners, some opened. Men's wearing apparel exposed. Mantelpiece, R., in disorder. At back double doors (ajar) leading to another room. Door, L., leading to hall and front door.]

[TIME. Evening in August.]

[ALBERT SHAWN is reclining on the sofa, fully dressed, but obviously ill: an overcoat has been drawn over his legs. A conspicuous object is a magnificent light purple dressing-gown thrown across a chair.]

[Door bangs off. Enter ILAM CARVE in his shirt sleeves, hurriedly. SHAWN feebly tries to get up.]

CARVE. Now, don't move. Remember you're a sick man, and forget you're a servant.

(SHAWN shivers. CARVE, about to put on his dressing-gown, changes his mind, and wraps it round SHAWN as well as he can. CARVE then puts on an oldish coat.)

SHAWN. (Feebly.) You've been very quick, sir.

CARVE. I found a red lamp only three doors off. He'll be along in half a minute.

SHAWN. Did you explain what it was, sir?

CARVE. (Genially.) How could I explain what it was, you fool, when I don't know? I simply asked to see the doctor, and I told him there was a fellow-creature suffering at No. 126, and would he come at once. "126?" he said, "126 has been shut up for years."

SHAWN. (Trying to smile.) What did you say, sir?

CARVE. I said (articulating with clearness) a hundred and twenty-six and ran off. Then he yelled out after me that he'd come instantly.... I say, Shawn, we're discovered. I could tell that from his sudden change of tone. I bet the entire street knows that the celebrated Me has arrived at last. I feel like a criminal already, dashed if I don't! I wish we'd gone to a hotel now. (Walks about.) I say, did you make up the bed?

SHAWN. I was just doing it, sir.

CARVE. But what about sheets and so on?

SHAWN. I bought some this morning, ready hemmed, sir, with those and the travelling rug

CARVE. Well, don't you think you could work your passage out to the bed? With my help?

SHAWN. Me in your bed, sir!

CARVE. (Genially bullying.) Keep on in that tone and I'll give you the sack on the spot. Now then. Try, before the doctor comes. (Bell rings.)

SHAWN. The bell, sir, excuse me.

CARVE. Confound

(Exit CARVE.)

(SHAWN coughs and puts a handkerchief to his mouth. CARVE returns immediately with DR. PASCOE.)

PASCOE. (Glancing round quickly.) This the patient? (Goes to SHAWN, and looks at him. Then, taking a clinical thermometer from his pocket and wiping it; with marked respect.) Allow me to put this under your tongue for half a minute. (Having done so, he takes SHAWN'S wrist and, looking at his watch, counts the patient's pulse. Then turning to CARVE, in a low curt voiced) When did this begin?

CARVE. Just now. That is, he only began to complain about six o'clock. We arrived in London this morning from Madrid.

PASCOE. (Reading thermometer.) Temperature 104-1/2. Pulse is 140 and weak. I must have some boiling water.

CARVE. (At a loss.) What for?

PASCOE. What for? For a poultice.

CARVE. (Helplessly.) But there isn't any ... we've nothing except this spirit-lamp. (Pointing to lamp on table.)

PASCOE. No women in the house?

CARVE. (With humour that the doctor declines to see.) Not one.

PASCOE. (Controlling his exasperation.) Never mind. I'll run round to the surgery and get my hypodermic. (To SHAWN, reassuringly and deferentially.) I shall be back at once, Mr. Carve. (To CARVE, near door.) Keep your master well covered up, I suppose you can do that?

(Exit.)

CARVE. Shawn, my poor fellow, he takes you for the illustrious Ilam Carve. This is what comes of me rushing out in shirt sleeves. (Gesture of despair.) I can't explain it to him.

SHAWN. But -

CARVE. It's all right. You'll be infinitely better looked after, you know, and I shall be saved from their infernal curiosity.

SHAWN. It's only this, sir. I was half-expecting a young lady to-night, sir (very feebly). At least, I believe she's young.

CARVE. Shawn, I've always suspected you were a bad lot. Now I know. I also know why you were so devilish anxious to put me to bed early. What am I to say to this young lady on your behalf?

(SHAWN worse, too ill to answer. Pause. Re-enter DR. PASCOE, very rapidly, with a large tumbler half-full of hot liquid.)

PASCOE. You may say I've been quick. (As he bends down to SHAWN, addressing CARVE.) Get me a wine glass of clean cold water. (To SHAWN.) Now, please. I want you to drink a little brandy and water. (SHAWN makes no response.) By Jove! (The doctor pours some of the brandy and water down SHAWN'S throat.)

CARVE. (Who has been wandering about vaguely.) I don't think we've got a wine glass. There's a cup, but I suppose that isn't medical enough.

PASCOE. (Taking a syringe from his pocket and unscrewing it.) Pour some water in it. (CARVE obeys.) Now, hold it.

CARVE. (Indicating syringe.) What is this device? PASCOE. This device? I'm going to get some strychnine into him by injection. Steady with that cup, now!

(Pascoe drops a tablet into the syringe and screws it up again, draws a little water up into the syringe and shakes the syringe. Then he goes to SHAWN to make the injection, on the top side of the patient's forearm. CARVE still holds the cup out mechanically.)

PASCOE. I've done with that cup.

CARVE. (Putting the cup down.) Might I ask what's the matter with him?

PASCOE. Pneumonia is the matter.

(Noise of some one in the hall.)

CARVE. (Startled.) Surely that's some one in the hall.

PASCOE. Keep perfectly calm, my man. It's my assistant. I left the door open on purpose for him. He's got the poultice and things. (In a loud voice as he finishes the injection.) Come along, come along there. This way.

(Enter EDWARD HORNING with poultice, lint, bandages, etc.)

PASCOE. Found the antiphlogistine?

EDWARD. Yes. (He looks at patient, and exchanges a glance with PASCOE.)

PASCOE. Where's the bedroom?

CARVE. There's one there. (Pointing to double doors.)

PASCOE. (To HORNING.) We'll get him into bed now. (To CARVE.) Bed ready?

CARVE. Yes. I, I think he was just making it up.

PASCOE. (Startled.) Does he make up his own bed?

CARVE. (Perceiving the mistake, but resuming his calm.) Always.

PASCOE. (Controlling his astonishment; looking through double doors and opening them wider. To HORNING.) Yes, this will do. Put those things down here a minute while we lift him.

(PASCOE and HORNING then carry the inanimate form of SHAWN into the room behind, while CARVE hovers about uselessly.)

CARVE. Can I do anything?

PASCOE. (Indicating a chair furthest away from the double doors.) You see that chair?

CARVE. I see it.

PASCOE. Go and sit on it.

(Exeunt PASCOE and HORNING, back, closing double door's.)

(After walking about, CARVE sits down on another chair. A bell rings twice. He pays no attention. Then enter JANET CANNOT, L. CARVE jumps up, but is inarticulate, though very favourably interested.)

JANET. (Smiling sympathetically.) I rang twice.

CARVE. The bell must be out of order.

JANET. I couldn't be sure, but I don't think it's the bell that's out of order.

CARVE. Oh! You think I'm out of order.

JANET. No. I was thinking that you'd only just come into the house, all you famous folk, and you hadn't quite got it straight yet, as it were. (Looking vaguely at room.)

CARVE. All we famous folk?

JANET. Well I don't know myself about that sort of thing.

CARVE. What sort of thing?

JANET. Picture-painting, isn't it? I mean real pictures done by hand, coloured - CARVE. Ah, yes.

JANET. (After a slight pause.) It struck me all of a sudden, while I was waiting at the door, that it might have been left open on purpose.

CARVE. The front door? On purpose? What for?

JANET. Oh, for some one particular to walk in without any fuss. So in I stepped.

CARVE. You're the young lady that Mr. Shawn's expecting (Going towards passage.)

JANET. (Stopping him.) It's shut now. You don't want everybody walking in, do you?

CARVE. (Looking at JANET with pleasure.) So you're the young lady, Mrs., Miss

JANET. (Ignoring his question.) Was it a message you had for me?

CARVE. No, no. Not a message.... But, the fact is, we're rather upset here for the moment.

JANET. Yes. Illness.

CARVE. Now, if it isn't an indiscreet question, how did you know that there was illness?

JANET. I was standing looking at this house and wondering whether I shouldn't do better to go right back home there and then. But "No," I said, "I've begun, and I'll go through with it." Well, I was standing there when what should I see but a parlour maid pop up from the area steps next door, and she says to me over the railings, "The doctor's just been." Just like that, excited. So I said, "Thank you, miss." I hope it's nothing serious?

CARVE. Pneumonia.

JANET. Pneumonia. What a mercy!

CARVE. Mercy?

JANET. If you look at it sensibly it's about the best illness anybody could have in hot weather like this. You've got to keep them warm. The weather does it for you. If it was typhoid now, and you'd got to keep them cool, that would be awkward. Not but it passes me how anybody can catch pneumonia in August.

CARVE. Coming over from the Continent.

JANET. Oh! the Continent. It's not Mr. Shawn that's ill?

CARVE. (Hesitating.) Mr. Shawn? Oh no, no! It's Ilam Carve.

JANET. (Half whispering. Awed.) Oh, him! Poor thing. And nobody but men in the house.

CARVE. And who told you that?

JANET. Well! (waves her hand to indicate the state of the room, smiling indulgently) I always feel sorry for gentlemen when they have to manage for themselves, even if they're well and hearty. But when it comes to illness, I can't bear to think about it. Still, everybody has their own notions of comfort. And I've no doubt he'll very soon be better.

CARVE. You think he will?

JANET. (Blandly cheerful.) As a general rule, you may say that people do get better. That's my experience. Of course sometimes they take a longish time. And now and then one dies, else what use would cemeteries be? But as a general rule they're soon over it. Now am I going to see Mr. Shawn, or shall I

CARVE. Well, if you could call again

JANET. You say you hadn't a message?

CARVE. Not precisely a message. But if you could call again

JANET. When?

CARVE. (Rather eagerly.) Any time. Any time. Soon.

JANET. Night after to-morrow?

CARVE. Why not morning?

JANET. Perhaps morning is safer. Thank you. Very well, then. Day after to-morrow.... I suppose Mr. Shawn has a rare fine situation here?

CARVE. (Shrugging his shoulders.) Nothing to complain of, if you ask me.

(JANET offers her hand quite simply. The double doors open, CARVE looks alarmed.)

JANET. Thank you very much. I think I can open the front door myself.

CARVE. I say, you won't forget?

JANET. Well, what do you think?

(Exit, L.)

(Enter DR. PASCOE through double doors.)

PASCOE. (At double doors, to HORNING invisible behind.) Then there's no reason why the nurse at Edith Grove shouldn't come along here.

HORNING. (Off.) Yes. She'll be free in an hour.

PASCOE. All right. I'll look in there.

HORNING. (Nervous.) What am I to do if his respiration

PASCOE. (Interrupting.) Don't worry. I'm not gone yet. I must just clean up my hypodermic. Shut those doors.

(HORNING obeys.)

CARVE. What's this about a nurse?

PASCOE. (Busy with syringe, water, and syringe-case.) I'm sending one in. (Ironically.) Do you see any objection?

CARVE. On the contrary, I should like him to be treated with every care. He's invaluable to me.

PASCOE. (Staggered.) Invaluable to you! Of course in my line of business I get used to meeting odd people

CARVE. (Recovering from his mistake.) But you think I carry oddness rather far?

PASCOE. The idea did pass through my mind.

CARVE. Nervousness, nothing but nervousness. I'm very nervous. And then, you know the saying, like master, like man.

PASCOE. (Indicating back room with a gesture; in a slightly more confidential tone as CARVE'S personal attractiveness gains on him.) Mr. Carve odd?

CARVE. Oh, very. Always was. Ever since I've known him. You remember his first picture at the Academy?

PASCOE. No, not exactly.

CARVE. Either you remember it exactly or you don't remember it at all. Life-size picture of a policeman blowing his whistle.

PASCOE. Yes; it must have been odd, that must.

CARVE. Not a bit. The oddness of the fellow

PASCOE. What 'fellow', your governor?

CARVE. (Nods.) His oddness came out in this way, although the thing had really a great success, from that day to this he's never painted another life-size picture of a policeman blowing his whistle.

PASCOE. I don't see anything very odd there

CARVE. Don't you? Well, perhaps you don't go in for art much. If you did, you'd know that the usual and correct thing for a painter who has made a great success with a life-size picture of a policeman blowing his whistle, is to keep on doing life-size pictures of a policeman blowing his whistle for ever and ever, so that the public can always count on getting from him a life-size picture of a policeman blowing his whistle.

PASCOE. I observe you are one of those comic valets. Nervousness again, no doubt.

CARVE. (Smiling and continuing.) Seeing the way he invariably flouted the public, it's always been a mystery to me how he managed to make a name, to say nothing of money.

PASCOE. Money! He must make pots. You say I don't go in for art much, but I always read the big sales at Christie's. Why, wasn't it that policeman picture that Lord Leonard Alcar bought for 2000 guineas last year?

CARVE. No, not Alcar. I think the bobby was last bought by Texel.

PASCOE. Texel? Who's Texel?

CARVE. Collector, United States, one of their kings, I'm told.

PASCOE. Oh, him! Controls all the ink in the United States.

CARVE. Really! That's what I should call influence. No. It was the "Pelicans feeding their Young" that Alcar bought. Four thousand. You're getting mixed up.

PASCOE. Perhaps I am. I know I'm constantly seeing Mr. Carve's name in connection with Lord Leonard Alcar's. It's a nice question which is the best known of the two.

CARVE. Then the governor really is famous in England? You see we never come to England.

PASCOE. Famous, I should think he was. Aren't they always saying he's the finest colourist since Titian? And look at his prices!

CARVE. Yes. I've looked at his prices. Titian's prices are higher, but Titian isn't what you'd call famous with the general public, is he? What I want to know is, is the governor famous among the general public?

PASCOE. Yes.

CARVE. About how famous should you say he is?

PASCOE. (Hesitating.) Well (abruptly) that's a silly question.

CARVE. No, it isn't. Is he as famous as, er, Harry Lauder?

PASCOE. (Shakes his head.) You mustn't go to extremes.

CARVE. Is he as famous as Harry Vardon?

PASCOE. Never heard of him.

CARVE. I only see these names in the papers. Is he as famous as Bernard Shaw?

PASCOE. Yes, I should say he was.

CARVE. Oh, well that's not so bad. Better than I thought! It's so difficult to judge where one is, er, personally concerned. Especially if you're never on the spot.

PASCOE. So it's true Mr. Carve never comes to England?

CARVE. Why should he come to England? He isn't a portrait painter. It's true he owns this house, but surely that isn't sufficient excuse for living in a place like England?

PASCOE. Of course, if you look at it like that, there's no particular attractiveness in England that I've ever seen. But that answer wouldn't satisfy Redcliffe Gardens. Redcliffe Gardens is persuaded that there must be a special reason.

CARVE. Well, there is.

PASCOE. (Interested, in spite of himself.) Indeed!

CARVE. (Confidentially.) Have a cigarette? (Offering case.)

PASCOE. (Staggered anew, but accepting.) That's a swagger case.

CARVE. Oh! (Calmly.) He gave it me.

PASCOE. Really?

CARVE. Well, you see we're more like brothers, been together so long. He gives me his best suits too. Look at this waistcoat. (Motions the hypnotised PASCOE to take a chair. They light their cigarettes.)

(Enter HORNING.)

PASCOE. (Somewhat impatient.) He's not worse already?

HORNING. Where's that brandy and water?

PASCOE. Be careful. He's had about enough of that.

HORNING. Seeing I've had no dinner yet, I thought it might suit me. (Exit with tumbler.)

PASCOE. (To Carve with renewed eagerness.) So there is a special reason why you keep out of England.

CARVE. Yes, shyness.

PASCOE. How, shyness?

CARVE. Just simple shyness. Shyness is a disease with the governor, a perfect disease.

PASCOE. But everyone's shy. The more experience I get the more convinced I am that we're all shy. Why, you were shy when you came to fetch me!

CARVE. Did you notice it?

PASCOE. Of course. And I was shy when I came in here. I was thinking to myself, "Now I'm going to see the great Ilam Carve actually in the flesh," and I was shy. You'd think my profession would have cured me of being shy, but not a bit. Nervous disease, of course! Ought to be treated as such. Almost universal. Besides, even if he is shy, your governor, even if he's a hundredfold shy, that's no reason for keeping out of England. Shyness is not one of those diseases you can cure by change of climate.

CARVE. Pardon me. My esteemed employer's shyness is a special shyness. He's only shy when he has to play the celebrity. So long as people take him for no one in particular he's quite all right. For instance, he's never shy with me. But instantly people approach him as the celebrity, instantly he sees in the eye of the beholder any consciousness of being in the presence of a toff, then he gets desperately shy, and his one desire is to be alone at sea or to be buried somewhere deep in the bosom of the earth. (PASCOE laughs.) What are you laughing at? (CARVE also laughs.)

PASCOE. Go on, go on. I'm enjoying it.

CARVE. No, but seriously! It's true what I tell you. It amounts almost to a tragedy in the brilliant career of my esteemed. You see now that England would be impossible for him as a residence. You see, don't you?

PASCOE. Quite.

CARVE. Why, even on the Continent, in the big towns and the big hotels, we often travel incognito for safety. It's only in the country districts that he goes about under his own name.

PASCOE. So that he's really got no friends?

CARVE. None, except a few Italian and Spanish peasants and me.

PASCOE. Well, well! It's an absolute mania then, this shyness.

CARVE. (Slightly hurt.) Oh, not so bad as that! And then it's only fair to say he has his moments of great daring, you may say rashness.

PASCOE. All timid people are like that.

CARVE. Are they? (Musing.) We're here now owing to one of his moments of rashness.

PASCOE. Indeed!

CARVE. Yes. We met an English lady in a village in Andalusia, and, well, of course, I can't tell you everything but she flirted with him and he flirted with her.

PASCOE. Under his own name?

CARVE. Yes. And then he proposed to her. I knew all along it was a blunder.

PASCOE. (Ironic.) Did you?

CARVE. Yes. She belonged to the aristocracy, and she was one of those amateur painters that wander about the Continent by themselves, you know.

PASCOE. And did she accept?

CARVE. Oh yes. They got as far as Madrid together, and then all of a sudden my esteemed saw that he had made a mistake.

PASCOE. And what then?

CARVE. We fled the country. We hooked it. The idea of coming to London struck him, just the caprice of a man who's lost his head and here we are.

PASCOE. (After a pause.) He doesn't seem to me from the look of him to be a man who'd, shall we say? strictly avoided women.

CARVE. (Startled, with a gesture towards back.) Him?

(PASCOE nods.)

Really! Confound him! Now I've always suspected that; though he manages to keep his goings-on devilish quiet.

PASCOE. (Rising.) It occurs to me, my friend, that I'm listening to too much. But you're so persuasive.

CARVE. It's such a pleasure to talk freely, for once in a way.

PASCOE. Freely is the word.

CARVE. Oh! He won't mind!

PASCOE. (In a peculiar tone.) It's quite possible!

(Enter HORNING.)

HORNING. (To Carve.) I say, it's just occurred to me, Mr. Carve hasn't been digging or gardening or anything, I suppose, and then taken cold after?

CARVE. Digging? Oh no. He must have got a bad chill on the steamer. Why?

HORNING. Nothing. Only his hands and finger-nails are so rough.

CARVE. (After thinking.) Oh, I see! All artists are like that. Messing about with paints and acids and things. Look at my hands.

PASCOE. But are you an artist too?

CARVE. (Recovering himself, calmly.) No, no.

PASCOE. (To Horning.) How's he going on?

HORNING. (Shrugs his shoulders.) I'm sure the base of both lungs is practically solid.

PASCOE. Well, we can't do more than we have done, my boy.

HORNING. He'll never pull through.

PASCOE. (Calmly.) I should certainly be surprised if he did.

CARVE. (Astounded.) But, but

PASCOE. But what?

CARVE. You don't mean to say. Why, he's a strong healthy man!

PASCOE. Precisely. Not very unusual for your strong healthy man to die of pneumonia in twenty-four hours. You ought to know, at your age, that it's a highly dangerous thing to be strong and healthy. (Turning away.) I'll have another look at him before I go.

CARVE. (Extremely perturbed.) But this is ridiculous. I simply don't know what I shall do without that man.

[The stage is darkened for a few moments to indicate passage of time.]


## ACT I SCENE II

[TIME. The next morning but one. Slightly less disorder in the room.]

[CARVE and PASCOE are together, the latter ready to leave.]

CARVE. Will there have to be an inquest?

PASCOE. Inquest? Of course not.

CARVE. It's some relief to know that. I couldn't have faced a coroner.

PASCOE. (Staring at him.) Perfectly ordinary case.

CARVE. That's what you call perfectly ordinary, is it? A man is quite well on Tuesday afternoon, and dead at 4 a.m. on Thursday morning. (Looking at his watch.) My watch has stopped.

PASCOE. (With fierce sarcasm.) One of those cheap German watches, I suppose, that stop when you don't wind them up! It's a singular thing that when people stay up all night they take it for granted their watches are just as excited as they are. Look here, you'll be collapsing soon. When did you have anything to eat last?

CARVE. Almost half an hour ago. Two sausages that were sent in yesterday for the nurse.

PASCOE. She's gone?

CARVE. Oh yes.

PASCOE. Well, take my advice. Try to get some sleep now. You've had no reply from the relatives, the auctioneer cousin, what's his Christian name, Cyrus?

CARVE. No, I, I didn't telegraph, I forgot

PASCOE. Well, upon my soul! I specially reminded you yesterday afternoon.

CARVE. I didn't know the address.

PASCOE. Ever heard of the London Directory? You'd better run out and wire instantly. You don't seem to realize that the death of a man like Ilam Carve will make something of a stir in the world. And you may depend on it that whether they'd quarrelled or not, Cyrus Carve will want to know why he wasn't informed of the illness at once. You've let yourself in for a fine row, and well you deserve it.

CARVE. (After a few paces.) See here, doctor. I'm afraid there's been some mistake. (Facing him nervously.)

PASCOE. What?

CARVE. I - I

(Bell rings.)

PASCOE. (Firmly.) Listen to me, my man. There's been no sort of mistake. Everything has been done that could be done. Don't you get ideas into your head. Lie down and rest. You're done up, and if you aren't careful you'll be ill. I'll communicate with Cyrus Carve. I can telephone, and while I'm about it I'll ring up the registrar too, he'll probably send a clerk round.

CARVE. Registrar?

PASCOE. Registrar of deaths. There'll be all kinds of things to attend to. (Moving to go out.)

(Bell rings again.)

CARVE. (As if dazed.) Is that the front door bell?

PASCOE. (Drily.) Quite possibly! I'll open it.

(Exit.)

(CARVE, alone, makes a gesture of despair. Re-enter PASCOE with CYRUS CARVE.)

PASCOE. (As they enter.) Yes, very sudden, very sudden. There were three of us, a nurse, my assistant, and myself. This is Mr. Shawn, the deceased's valet.

CYRUS. Morning. (Looks round at disorder of room contemptuously.) Pigstye!... My name is Cyrus Carve. I'm your late master's cousin and his only relative. You've possibly never heard of me.

CARVE. (Curtly.) Oh yes, I have! You got up a great quarrel when you were aged twelve, you and he.

CYRUS. Your manner isn't very respectful, my friend. However you may have treated my cousin, be good enough to remember you're not my valet.

CARVE. How did you get to know about it?

CYRUS. I suppose he forbade you to send for me, eh? (Pause.) Eh?

CARVE. (Jumping at this suggestion.) Yes.

PASCOE. So that was it.

CYRUS. (Ignoring PASCOE.) Ha! Well, since you're so curious, I saw it a quarter of an hour ago in a special edition of a halfpenny rag; I was on my way to the office. (Showing paper.) Here you are! The Evening Courier. Quite a full account of the illness. You couldn't send for me, but you could chatter to some journalist.

CARVE. I've never spoken to a journalist in my life.

CYRUS. Then how?

PASCOE. It's probably my assistant. His brother is something rather important on the Courier, and he may have telephoned to him. It's a big item of news, you know, Mr. Carve.

CYRUS. (Drily.) I imagine so. Where is the body?

PASCOE. Upstairs. (Moving towards door.)

CYRUS. Thanks. I will go alone.

PASCOE. Large room at back, first floor.

(Exit CYRUS, L.)

I think I'd prefer to leave you to yourselves now. Of course, Mr. Carve will do all that's necessary. You might give him my card, and tell him I'm at his service as regards signing the death certificate and so on. (Handing card.)

CARVE. (Taking card perfunctorily.) Very well. Then you're going? PASCOE. Yes. (Moves away and then suddenly puts out his hand, which CARVE takes.) Want a word of advice?

CARVE. I - I ought

PASCOE. If I were you I should try to get something better than valeting. It's not your line. You may have suited Ilam Carve, but you'd never suit an ordinary employer. You aren't a fool, not by any means.

(CARVE shrugs his shoulders.)

(Exit PASCOE, L. Door shuts off.)

(Re-enter CYRUS immediately after the door shuts.)

CARVE. (To himself.) Now for it! (To CYRUS). Well?

CYRUS. Well what?

CARVE. Recognize your cousin?

CYRUS. Of course a man of forty-five isn't like a boy of twelve, but I think I may say I should have recognized him anywhere.

CARVE. (Taken aback.) Should you indeed. (A pause.) And so you're Cyrus, the little boy that kicked and tried to bite in that historic affray of thirty years ago.

CYRUS. Look here, I fancy you and I had better come to an understanding at once. What salary did my cousin pay you for your remarkable services?

CARVE. What salary?

CYRUS. What salary?

CARVE. Eighty pounds a year.

CYRUS. When were you last paid?

CARVE. I - I

CYRUS. When were you last paid?

CARVE. The day before yesterday.

CYRUS. (Taking a note and gold from his pocket-book and pocket.) Here's seven pounds, a month's wages in lieu of notice. It's rather more than a month's wages, but I can't do sums in my head just now. (Holding out money.)

CARVE. But listen

CYRUS. (Commandingly.) Take it.

(CARVE obeys.)

Pack up and be out of this house within an hour.

CARVE. I

CYRUS. I shall not argue.... Did your master keep his private papers and so on in England or somewhere on the Continent, what bank?

CARVE. What bank? He didn't keep them in any bank.

CYRUS. Where did he keep them then?

CARVE. He kept them himself.

CYRUS. What, travelling?

CARVE. Yes. Why not?

CYRUS. (With a "tut-tut" noise to indicate the business man's mild scorn of the artist's method's.) Whose is this luggage?

CARVE. Mine.

CYRUS. All of it?

CARVE. That is

CYRUS. Come now, is it his or is it yours? Now be careful.

CARVE. His. (Angrily, as CYRUS roughly handles a box.) Now then, mind what you're about! Those are etching things.

CYRUS. I shall mind what I'm about. And what's this?

CARVE. That's a typewriter.

CYRUS. I always thought artists couldn't stand typewriting machines.

CARVE. That was his servant's.

CYRUS. Yours, you mean?

CARVE. Yes, I mean mine.

CYRUS. Then why don't you say so? What do you want a typewriter for?

CARVE. (Savagely.) What the devil has that got to do with you?

CYRUS. (Looking up calmly from the examination of a dispatch box.) If you can't keep a civil tongue in your head I'll pitch you down the front-door steps and your things after you.

CARVE. I've got something to tell you

CYRUS. Silence, and answer my questions! Are his papers in this dispatch box?

CARVE. Yes.

CYRUS. Where are his keys?

CARVE. (Slowly drawing bunch of keys from his pocket.) Here.

CYRUS. (Taking them.) So you keep his keys?

CARVE. Yes.

CYRUS. (Opening dispatch box.) Wear his clothes too, I should say!

(CARVE sits down negligently and smiles.)

CYRUS. (As he is examining papers in box.) What are you laughing at?

CARVE. I'm not laughing. I'm smiling. (Rising and looking curiously at box.) There's nothing there except lists of securities and pictures and a few oddments, passports and so on.

CYRUS. There appears to be some money. I'm glad you've left that. Quite a lot, in fact. (Showing notes.)

CARVE. Here, steady! There's twelve thousand francs there besides some English notes. That's mine.

CYRUS. Yours, eh? He was taking care of it for you, no doubt?

CARVE. (Hesitating.) Yes.

CYRUS. When you can furnish me with his receipt for the deposit, my man, it shall be handed to you. Till then it forms part of the estate. (Looking at a packet of letters.) "Alice Rowfant."

CARVE. And those letters are mine too.

CYRUS. (Reading.) "My dearest boy". Were you Lady Alice Rowfant's dearest boy? Anyhow, we'll burn them.

CARVE. So long as you burn them I don't mind.

CYRUS. Indeed! (Continues to examine papers, cheque foils, etc. Then opens a document.)

CARVE. Oh! Is that still there? I thought it was destroyed.

CYRUS. Do you know what it is?

CARVE. Yes. It's a will that was made in Venice I don't know how long ago, just after your aunt died and you had that appalling and final shindy by correspondence about the lease of this house. Everything is left for the establishment of an International Gallery of Painting and Sculpture in London, and you're the sole executor, and you get a legacy of five pounds for your trouble.

CYRUS. Yes.... So I see. No doubt my cousin imagined it would annoy me.

CARVE. He did.

CYRUS. He told you so?

CARVE. He said it would be one in the eye for you and he wondered whether you'd decline the executorship.

CYRUS. Well, my man, I may tell you at once that I shall not renounce probate. I never expected a penny from my cousin. I always assumed he'd do something silly with his money, and I'm relieved to find it's no worse. In fact, the idea of a great public institution in London being associated with my family is rather pleasant.

CARVE. But he meant to destroy that will long since.

CYRUS. (As he cons the will.) How do you know? Has he made a later will?

CARVE. No.

CYRUS. Well, then! Besides, I fail to see why you should be so anxious to have it destroyed. You come into eighty pounds a year under it.

CARVE. I was forgetting that.

CYRUS. (Reading.) "I bequeath to my servant, Albert Shawn, who I am convinced is a thorough rascal, but who is an unrivalled valet, courier, and factotum, the sum of eighty pounds a year for life, payable quarterly in advance, provided he is in my service at the time of my death."

(CARVE laughs shortly.)

You don't want to lose that, do you? Of course, if the term "thorough rascal" is offensive to you, you can always decline the money. (Folds up will and puts it in his pocket CARVE walks about.) Now where's the doctor?

CARVE. He's left his card. There it is.

CYRUS. He might have waited.

CARVE. Yes. But he didn't. His house is only three doors off.

CYRUS. (Looking at his watch.) I'll go in and see him about the certificate. Now you haven't begun to put your things together, and you've only got a bit over half an hour. In less than that time I shall be back. I shall want to look through your luggage before you leave.

CARVE. (Lightly.) Shall you?

CYRUS. By the way, you have a latchkey? (CARVE nods.) Give it me, please.

(CARVE surrenders latchkey.)

(CYRUS turns to go. As he is disappearing through the door, L., CARVE starts forward.)

CARVE. I say.

CYRUS. What now?

CARVE. (Subsiding weakly.) Nothing.

(Exit CYRUS. Sound of front door opening and of voices in hall.)

(Then re-enter CYRUS with JANET CANNOT.)

CYRUS. This is Mr. Albert Shawn. Shawn, a friend of yours.

(Exit L.)

CARVE. (Pleased.) Oh! You!

JANET. Good-morning. D'you know, I had a suspicion the other night that you must be Mr. Shawn?

CARVE. Had you? Well, will you sit down, er, I say (with a humorous mysterious air). What do you think of that chap? (Pointing in direction of hall.)

JANET. Who is it?

CARVE. It's Mr. Cyrus Carve. The great West End auctioneer.

(Sound of front-door shutting rather too vigorously.)

JANET. Well, I see no reason why he should look at me as if I'd insulted him.

CARVE. Did he?

JANET. "Good-morning," I said to him. "Excuse me, but are you Mr. Albert Shawn?" Because I wasn't sure, you know. And he looked.

CARVE. (After laughing.) The man is an ass.

JANET. Is he?

CARVE. Not content with being an ass merely, he is a pompous and a stupid ass. (Laughs again to himself.) Now there is something very important that he ought to know, and he wouldn't let me tell him. JANET. Really?

CARVE. Yes, very important. But no. He wouldn't let me tell him. And perhaps if I'd told him he wouldn't have believed me.

JANET. What did he do to stop you from telling him?

CARVE. (At a loss, vaguely.) I don't know. Wouldn't let me.

JANET. If you ask me, I should say the truth is, you didn't want to tell him.

CARVE. (Impressed.) Now I wonder if you're right.

JANET. Well, I don't quite see how anybody can stop anybody from talking. But even if he did, he can't stop you from writing to him.

CARVE. No, I'm hanged if I write to him!

JANET. Oh, well, that's a proof you didn't want to tell him.

CARVE. Perhaps it is. (After a burst of quiet laughter.) Pardon me. (Reflective.) I was only thinking what a terrific lark it will be.

JANET. If he never does get to know?

CARVE. If he never does get to know. If nobody ever gets to know. (Resolved.) No. I'll keep my mouth shut.

JANET. As a general rule, it's the best thing to do.

CARVE. You advise me to keep my mouth shut?

JANET. Not at all. I simply say, as a general rule it's the best thing to do. But this is no business of mine, and I'm sure I'm not inquisitive.

CARVE. (Solemnly.) He shall go his own way. (Pause.) And I'll go mine.

JANET. (Calmly indifferent.) That's settled, then.

CARVE. (Laughs again to himself, then controls his features.) And that being settled, the first thing I have to do is to apologize for my behaviour on Tuesday night.

JANET. Oh, not at all. Seeing how upset you were! And then I'm not sure whether I shouldn't have done the same thing myself in your place.

CARVE. Done the same yourself?

JANET. Well, I may be wrong, but it occurred to me your idea was that you'd like to have a look at me before giving yourself away, as it were. Of course, I sent you my photographs, but photographs aren't much better than gravestones, for being reliable, and some folks are prejudiced against matrimonial agencies, even when they make use of them. It's natural. Now I've got no such prejudice. If you want to get married you want to get married, and there you are. It's no use pretending you don't. And there's as much chance of being happy through a matrimonial agency as any other way. At least, that's what I think.

CARVE. (Collecting his wits.) Just so.

JANET. You may tell me that people who go to a matrimonial agency stand a chance of getting let in. Well, people who don't go to a matrimonial agency stand a chance of getting let in, too. Besides, I shouldn't give a baby a razor for a birthday present, and I shouldn't advise a young girl to go to a matrimonial agency. But I'm not a young girl. If it's a question of the male sex, I may say that I've been there before. You understand me?

CARVE. Quite.

JANET. Well, I think I told you pretty nearly everything important in my letter. Didn't I?

CARVE. Let me see now

JANET. I mean the one I sent to the office of the Matrimonial News.

CARVE. (Mechanically feeling in his pockets, pulling out papers and putting them back.) Where did I put it? Oh, perhaps it's in the pocket of another coat. (Goes to a coat of SHAWN'S hanging on inner knob of double doors, and empties all the pockets, bringing the contents, including a newspaper, to the table.)

JANET. (Picking up an envelope.) Yes, that's it, I can feel the photograph. You seem to keep things in the pockets of all your coats.

CARVE. If you knew what I've been through this last day or two

JANET. (Soothingly.) Yes, yes.

CARVE. I haven't had a quiet moment. Now (Reading letter.) "Dear Sir, in reply to your advertisement, I write to you with particulars of my case. I am a widow, aged thirty-two years"

JANET. And anybody that likes can see my birth certificate. That's what I call talking.

CARVE. My dear lady! (Continuing to read.) "Thirty-two years. My father was a jobbing builder, well known in Putney and Wandsworth. My husband was a rent collector and estate agent. He died four years ago of appendicitis (hesitating) caught"

JANET. Caused.

CARVE. I beg pardon, " - caused by accidentally swallowing a bristle out of his tooth-brush, the same being discovered at the operation. I am an orphan, a widow, and have no children. In consequence I feel very lonely, and my first experience not being distasteful, indeed the reverse, I am anxious to try again, provided I can meet with a sincere helpmeet of good family. I am the owner of the above house, rated at forty-five pounds a year, in one of the nicest streets in Putney, and I have private means of some three pounds a week, from brewery shares bringing in fifteen per cent. I will say nothing about my appearance, but enclose latest carte-de-visite photograph."

JANET. I had it taken on purpose.

CARVE. "As to my tastes, I will only say that as a general rule they are quiet. If the above seems in your line, I shall be obliged if you will write and send me particulars of yourself, with photographs. Yours truly, JANET CANNOT." Well, Mrs. Cannot, your letter is an absolute model.

JANET. I suppose you did get dozens?

CARVE. Well. By the way, what's this type-written thing in the envelope?

JANET. (Looking at it.) It looks like a copy of your answer.

CARVE. Oh!

JANET. If it isn't a rude question, Mr. Shawn, why do you typewrite your letters? It seems so, what shall I say? public.

CARVE. (Half to himself.) So that's the explanation of the typewriter.

JANET. (Puzzled.) I suppose it's because you're a private secretary.

CARVE. (Equally puzzled.) Private secretary! I shall we just glance through my reply? (Reads.) "My dear Mrs. Cannot, your letter inspires me with more confidence than any of the dozens of others I have received." (They look at each other, smiling.) "As regards myself, I should state at once that I am and have been for many years private secretary, indeed I may say almost companion, to the celebrated painter. Mr. Ilam Carve, whose magnificent pictures you are doubtless familiar with."

JANET. No, I'm not.

CARVE. Really. "We have been knocking about England together for longer than I care to remember, and I personally am anxious for a change. Our present existence is very expensive. I feel the need of a home and the companionship of just such a woman as yourself. Although a bachelor, I think I am not unfitted for the domestic hearth. My age is forty." That's a mistake of the typewriter.

JANET. Oh!

CARVE. Forty-five it ought to be.

JANET. Well, honestly, I shouldn't have thought it.

CARVE. "My age is forty-five. By a strange coincidence Mr. Carve has suggested to me that we set out for England to-morrow. At Dover I will telegraph you with a rendezvous. In great haste. Till then, my dear Mrs. Cannot, believe me," etc.

JANET. You didn't send a photograph.

CARVE. Perhaps I was afraid of prejudicing you in advance.

JANET. (Laughs.) Eh, Mr. Shawn! There's thousands of young gentlemen alive and kicking in London this minute that would give a great deal to be only half as good looking as you are. And so you're a bachelor?

CARVE. Oh, quite.

JANET. Two bachelors, as you say, knocking about Europe together. (CARVE laughs quietly but heartily to himself.) By the way, how is Mr. Carve? I hope he's better.

CARVE. Mr. Carve?...(Suddenly stops laughing.) Oh! (Lamely, casually.) He's dead!

JANET. (Stocked.) Dead? When?

CARVE. Early this morning.

JANET. (Rising.) And us chattering away like this. Why didn't you tell me at once, Mr. Shawn?

CARVE. I forgot for the moment. I wasn't thinking

JANET. Forgot?

CARVE. (Simply and sincerely, but very upset.) Now, Mrs. Cannot, I assure you I feel that man's death. I admit I had very little affection for him, certainly not much respect, but we'd been together a long time, and his death is a shock to me. Yes, really. But I've had to think so much about my own case and then a scene, a regular scene with Cyrus Carve. And then you coming. The fact is

JANET. (Sympathetically.) The fact is, you scarcely know what you're doing, my poor Mr. Shawn. You're on wires, that's what's the matter with you, hysteria. I know what it is as well as anybody. You'll excuse me saying so, but you're no ordinary man. You're one of these highly-strung people and you ought to take care of yourself. Well, I'll go now, and if it's mutually agreeable we might perhaps meet again in a month's time say.

CARVE. A month? But what am I to do with myself for a month? Do you know you're absolutely the only friend I've got in London, in England. We're never here. I'm an utter stranger. You can't leave me like that for a month, four weeks, four Sundays. I haven't the least idea what's going to happen to me.

JANET. The very best thing that can happen to you is bed. You go to bed and stop there for a couple of days. There's nothing like it.

CARVE. Yes, but where?

JANET. Why, here of course.

CARVE. I've got to be out of this place in half an hour, less. The fact is, Cyrus Carve has been extremely, er, pert. He's paid me a month's salary and I'm off at once. In under thirty minutes I shall be on the streets.

JANET. I never liked that man. Well, then, you must go to some nice respectable boarding-house.

CARVE. But I don't know any nice respectable boarding-house.

JANET. Oh! There are thousands and thousands in London. Look in the Telegraph.

CARVE. I haven't had a paper to-day.

JANET. Any day will do. They're in all the papers every day. What's this? (Taking up folded dirty newspaper and opening it.) Now, let's see. Well, what about this? "A beautiful private hotel of the highest class. Luxuriously furnished. Visitors' comfort studied. Finest position in London. Cuisine a speciality. Suitable for persons of superior rank. Bathroom. Electric light. Separate tables. No irritating extras. Single rooms from two and a half guineas. 250 Queen's Gate." Quite close by! (CARVE says nothing.) Perhaps that's a bit dear. Here's another. "Not a boarding-house. A magnificent mansion. Forty bedrooms by Waring. Superb public saloons by Maple. Parisian chef. Separate tables. Four bathrooms. Card-rooms. Billiard room. Vast lounge. Special sanitation. Young, cheerful, musical society. Bridge (small). Finest position in London. No irritating extras. Single rooms from two guineas." What about that?

CARVE. (Shakes his head.) I don't think I should fancy it.

JANET. I won't say but what two guineas a week is a lot.

CARVE. And I was thinking how cheap it was.

JANET. (Staring.) Well, of course, if you've got money to fling about.

CARVE. Upon my soul I don't know what money I have got.

JANET. It'll be just as well to find out before you get into the street.

CARVE. Let's see. Well, there's seven pounds (showing it.) and this (pulling silver and gold from another pocket). Not much is it? Sixteen shillings and sixpence. It's true I've an annuity of eighty pounds. I was forgetting that.

JANET. (Pleased.) Have you indeed?

CARVE. Yes. But an annuity isn't ready cash, is it?

JANET. (Picking up Shawn's pocket-book.) And this? This seems rather thick.

CARVE. I was forgetting that too. (Opens it and takes out many notes.)

JANET. My word! And you'd forgotten that! You ought to see a doctor.

CARVE. (Counting.) Twenty-one fives, and ten tens. That makes two hundred and five pounds. (Half to himself.) I always knew I was a bad lot, but where did I collar all that from? (To Janet.) I know what I shall do! I shall go to the Grand Babylon.

JANET. The Grand Babylon Hotel? But it's the dearest hotel in London.

CARVE. In the big towns we always went to the best hotel. It's cheapest in the end.

JANET. You're very persuasive, but you'll never make me believe you'll save money by staying at the Grand Babylon.

CARVE. (Rising and beginning to collect things, tries to fold up a pair of trousers.) Now, Mrs. Cannot, will you do me a favour?

JANET. You'll spoil these trousers.

CARVE. Will you come and lunch with me at the Grand Babylon to-morrow?

JANET. But I've never been in such a place in my life.

CARVE. Remember. You're my only friend. Will you come and lunch with me at the Grand Babylon to-morrow?

JANET. (Timidly.) I should like to. (Suddenly.) Here, give me those trousers, do! (She takes hold of one leg, CARVE retaining the other.)

(Enter CYRUS CARVE.)

CYRUS. Oh!

[CURTAIN.]

## ACT II SCENE I

[Private sitting-room at the Grand Babylon Hotel, Strand. Luxurious in the hotel manner. Telephone. Door, L., leading to corridor. Door, R. (up stage), leading to bedroom. Another door (not used) leading by a passage to bathroom.]

[TIME. About noon on the following day. ILAM CARVE and JANET are talking together.]

CARVE. I'm really delighted to see you.

JANET. (Examining his features.) But surely you're not feeling very well?

CARVE. I'm not. Perhaps it's these sleepless nights I've had.

JANET. You're shivering.

CARVE. I was wearing my dressing-gown. I nearly always do when I'm alone. Do you think you'd mind if I put it on again.

JANET. Do you mean to say you took it off because of me? (Seizing dressing-gown firmly.) Mr. Shawn, will you oblige me by getting-into this at once? (She helps him on with dressing-gown.) What a beauty!

CARVE. Yes. Cousin Cyrus thought so too. He didn't want me to bring it away. Still, I beat him on that point. (JANET arranges the collar.) Do you know, you do me good.

JANET. I should think so. I suppose when gentlemen live alone they're pretty nearly always unwell, as it were. If it isn't a cold, it's stomach, I expect. And truly, I'm not surprised, the way they go on! Now, will you sit down in that chair and keep your legs covered. August or no August! If you ask me, it's influenza you're sickening for. (Sound of distant orchestral.) Music?

CARVE. (Nodding and sitting down in easy chair.) Well, and what's the news from outside? I haven't stirred since yesterday noon.

JANET. Seems to me there's no news except your Mr. Carve's death.

CARVE. Really! Is it so much talked about as all that?

JANET. It's on all the posters, very big. All along Piccadilly and Trafalgar Square and the Strand the newspaper boys, and the newspaper old men too, are wearing it like aprons, as it were. I read the Telegraph myself. There was nearly a page of it in the Telegraph.

CARVE. (Staggered.) Nearly a page of it in the Telegraph!

JANET. Yes, besides a leading article. Haven't you

CARVE. I never read obituaries of artists in the papers.

JANET. Neither do I. But I should have thought you would.

CARVE. Well, they make me angry. Obituaries of archbishops aren't so bad. Newspapers seem to understand archbishops. But when they begin about artists, you cannot imagine the astounding nonsense they talk.

JANET. (Protesting against his heat.) Now! You're still all on wires. Why should that make you angry?

CARVE. What did the Telegraph say? Did you look at it?

JANET. Oh yes. It appears Mr. Carve was a very eccentric person, avoiding society and so on.

CARVE. (Resentful.) Eccentric! There you are! He wasn't eccentric in the least. The only society he avoided was the society of gaping fools.

JANET. Well, I'm just telling you what it said. Then, let me see, what else did it say? Oh! It said the sole question was whether Mr. Carve was the greatest painter since Velasquez, is that how you pronounce it? or whether he was the greatest painter that ever lived.

CARVE. (Interested.) Really! It said that?

JANET. (Nodding.) You ought to read it.

CARVE. Upon my soul I think I must. (Attempts to rise.)

JANET. Now, please, don't move. What is it you want?

CARVE. I was only going to telephone and have the daily papers sent up.

JANET. Where is the telephone?

CARVE. (Pointing.) There.

JANET. So they've put a telephone in your room?

CARVE. Telephone in every room.

JANET. (Going to telephone.) Can I telephone for you? I never have telephoned, and I should like to. How do you do it?

CARVE. Just take that thing off the hook and talk into it. (JANET gingerly obeys.) It won't explode.

JANET. What am I to say?

CARVE. Tell them to send me up the daily papers at once.

JANET. All?

CARVE. Yes.

JANET. But will they?

CARVE. Certainly.

JANET. (Into telephone.) Please will you send up all the daily papers at once.

CARVE. Thanks very much. Now you can hang it up again.

JANET. So this is the Grand Babylon Hotel? Well it's a queer place. (Her eyes rove round the room.)

CARVE. What are you looking for?

JANET. To speak plainly, I was looking for the bed. I must say I was rather surprised when the young man at the desk said I was to go up to your room.... But really, every thing's so nicely arranged.... I suppose it's one of those folding beds that turn into bookcases and things?

CARVE. (Laughs.) No. This is my sitting-room.

JANET. Your sitting-room? (Pointing to door, R.) Then that's the bedroom?

CARVE. Yes.

JANET. (Pointing to another door.) And what's that?

CARVE. That's one way to my bathroom. In a big hotel I always take a suite, you know. It's so much more comfortable.

JANET. Isn't it rather expensive?

CARVE. To tell you the truth, I didn't ask the price.

(Knock at door.)

JANET. (Charmingly tart.) I suppose it's what you call "cheapest in the end." CARVE. Come in.

(Enter PAGE with a pile of papers.)

CARVE. Thanks! Give them to me.

(Exit PAGE.)

JANET. Well, I never! It's like magic.

CARVE. Now let's just glance at these chaps. (Unfolding a paper.)

JANET. Shall I help you?

CARVE. Why? Here's black borders and a heading across two columns! "Death of England's greatest painter," "Irreparable loss to the world's art," "Our readers will be shocked" Are they all like that? (More and more astonished; takes another paper.) "Sad death of a great genius."

JANET. (Handing him still another paper.) And this.

CARVE. "London's grief." "The news will come as a personal blow to every lover of great painting." But, but, I'd no notion of this. (Half to himself.) It's terrible.

JANET. Well, perhaps always living with him you wouldn't realize how important he was, would you? (Distant music begins again, a waltz tune.)

CARVE. (Reading.) "Although possibly something of a poseur in his choice of subjects...." The fellow's a fool. Poseur indeed!

JANET. Look at this. "Europe in mourning."

CARVE. Well, well.

JANET. What is that music?

CARVE. London's grief. It's the luncheon orchestra downstairs.

(Telephone bell rings.)

CARVE. Never mind it. Let 'em ring. I understand now why journalists and so on have been trying all day to see me. Honestly I'm, I'm staggered.

(Telephone bell continues to ring.)

JANET. It's a funny notion of comfort having a telephone in every room. How long will it keep on like that?

CARVE. I'll stop it. (Rising.)

JANET. No, no. (Going to telephone and taking receiver.) Yes? What's the matter? (Listens. To CARVE.) Oh, what do you think? Father Looe and his sister, Miss Honoria Looe, want to see you.

CARVE. Father Looe? Never heard of him.

JANET. Oh, but you must have heard of him. He's the celebrated Roman Catholic preacher. He's a beautiful man. I heard him preach once on the Sins of Society.

CARVE. Would you mind saying I'm not at home?

JANET. (Obviously disappointed.) Then won't you see him?

CARVE. Did you want to see him?

JANET. I should like just to have had a look at him close to, as it were.

CARVE. (Gallantly.) Then you shall. Tell them to send him up, will you?

JANET. And am I to stay here?

CARVE. Of course.

JANET. Well, if anybody had told me this time last week (Into telephone.) Please ask them to come up.

CARVE. Perhaps with your being here I shan't be quite so shy.

JANET. Shy! Are you shy? It said in the Telegraph that Mr. Carve was painfully shy.

CARVE. (Protesting.) Painfully! Who told them that, I should like to know?

JANET. Now shyness is a thing I simply can't understand. I'm never shy. And you don't strike me as shy, far from it.

CARVE. It's very curious. I haven't felt a bit shy with you.

JANET. Nobody ever is shy with me.... (Ironically.) I must say I'd give something to see you shy.

(Enter FATHER LOOE and HONORIA LOOE, announced by PAGE.)

LOOE. (Stopping near door, at a loss.) Pardon me, Mr. Shawn, Mr. Albert Shawn?

CARVE. (Rising, perturbed.) Yes.

LOOE. This is your room?

CARVE. Yes.

LOOE. I'm afraid there's some mistake. I was given to understand that you were the, er, valet of the late Mr. Ilam Carve.

HONORIA. Yes. Mr. Cyrus Carve told us

JANET. (Coming to CARVE'S rescue as he remains speechless, very calmly.) Now there's another trick of Mr. Cyrus Carve's! Valet indeed! Mr. Shawn was Mr. Carve's secretary and almost companion.

LOOE. Ten thousand apologies. Ten thousand apologies. I felt sure

CARVE. Please sit down. (With special gallantry towards HONORIA.)

JANET. And will you sit down too, Mr. Shawn? (To the LOOES.) He's not at all well. That's why he's wearing his dressing-gown.

CARVE. (Introducing.) My friend, Mrs. Janet Cannot.

LOOE. Now, Mr. Shawn, if you knew anything about me, if you have heard me preach, if you have read any of my books, you are probably aware that I am a man who goes straight to the point, hating subtleties. In connection with your late employer's death a great responsibility is laid upon me, and I have come to you for information, information which I have failed to obtain either from Mr. Cyrus Carve, or the doctor, or the nurse.... Was Mr. Carve a Catholic?

CARVE. A Catholic?

LOOE. He came of a Catholic family did he not?

CARVE. Yes, I believe so.

LOOE. The cousin, Mr. Cyrus Carve, I regret to say, denies the faith of his childhood, denies it, I also regret to say, with a vivacity that amounts almost to bad manners. In fact, he was extremely rude to me when I tried to give him some idea of the tremendous revival of Catholicism which is the outstanding feature of intellectual life in England to-day.

CARVE. Ilam Carve was not a Catholic.

LOOE. Mind, I do not ask if he died in the consolations of the faith. I know that he did not. I have learnt that it occurred to neither you nor the doctor nor the nurse to send for a priest. Strange omission. But not the fault of the dying man.

CARVE. Ilam Carve was not a Catholic.

LOOE. Then what was he?

CARVE. Nothing in particular.

LOOE. Then I claim him. Then I claim him.... Honoria!

CARVE. (In a new tone..) Look here, what's all this about?

LOOE. (Rising.) I will tell you at once what it is about, Mr. Shawn. There is a question of Ilam Carve being buried in Westminster Abbey.

CARVE. (Thunderstruck.) Buried in Westminster Abbey?

LOOK. Lady Leonard Alcar has consulted me about the matter. I may say that I have the honour to be her spiritual director. Probably you know that Lord Leonard Alcar owns the finest collection of Ilam Carve's pictures in Europe.

JANET. I've often wondered who it is that settles whether people shall be buried in the Abbey or not. So it's Lady Leonard Alcar!

LOOE. Not exactly! Not exactly! But Lady Leonard Alcar is a great lady. She has vast influence. The most influential convert to Catholicism of the last thirty years. She is aunt to no less than four dukes, and Lord Leonard is uncle to two others.

CARVE. (Ironically.) I quite see.

LOOE. (Eagerly.) You see, don't you? Her advice on these matters carries enormous weight. A suggestion from her amounts to, to

CARVE. A decree absolute.

JANET. (Simply.) Is she what they call the ruling classes?

LOOE. (Bows.) Lady Leonard and I have talked the matter over, and I pointed out to her that if this great genius was a member of the Church of England and if the sorrowing nation at large deems him worthy of the supreme honour of a national funeral, then by all means let him be buried in the Abbey. But if he was a Catholic, then I claim him for Westminster Cathedral, that magnificent fane which we have raised as a symbol of our renewed vitality. Now, was he a member of the Church of England?

CARVE. (Loudly.) Decidedly not.

LOOE. Good! Then I claim him. I detest casuistry and I claim him. I have only one other question. You knew him well, intimately, for many years. On your conscience, Mr. Shawn, what interment in your opinion would he himself have preferred?

JANET. (After a pause.) It wouldn't make much difference to him either way, would it?

CARVE. (With an outburst.) The whole thing is preposterous.

LOOE. (Ignoring the outburst.) My course seems quite clear. I shall advise Lady Leonard

CARVE. Don't you think you're rather young to be in sole charge of this country?

LOOE. (Smoothly.) My dear sir, I am nothing but a humble priest who gives counsel when counsel is sought. And I may say that in this affair of the interment of our great national painter, there are other influences than mine. For instance, my sister, Honoria, who happens also to be president of the Ladies' Water Colour Society (gesture of alarm from CARVE) my sister has a great responsibility. She is the favourite niece of (Whispers in CARVE'S ear.) Consequently (Makes an impressive pause.)

HONORIA. You see my uncle is a bachelor and I keep house for him. Anselm used to live with us too, until he left the Church.

LOOE. Until I joined the Church, Honoria. Now Honoria wishes to be perfectly fair; she entirely realizes her responsibility; and that is why she has come with me to see you.

JANET. (Benignantly.) So that's how these things are decided! I see I'd got quite a wrong notion of politics and so on.

HONORIA. Oh, Mr. Shawn}
and } (Together.)
JANET. My idea was}

JANET. I beg your pardon.

HONORIA. I beg yours.

JANET. Granted.

HONORIA. There's one question I should so like to ask you, Mr. Shawn. In watercolours did Mr. Carve use Chinese white freely or did he stick to transparent colour, like the old English school? I wonder if you understand me?

CARVE. (Interested.) He used Chinese white like anything.

HONORIA. Oh! I'm so glad. You remember that charming water-colour of the Venetian gondolier in the Luxembourg. We had a great argument after we got home last Easter as to whether the oar was put in with Chinese white or just 'left out,' you know!

CARVE. Chinese white, of course. My notion is that it doesn't matter a fig how you get effects so long as you do get them.

HONORIA. And that was his notion too? (Telephone bell rings, JANET answers it.)

CARVE. His? Rather. You bet it was.

HONORIA. I'm so glad. I'm so glad. I knew I was right about Chinese white. Oh, Anselm, do let him be buried in the Abbey! Do let me suggest to uncle

LOOE. My dear girl, ask your conscience. Enthusiasm for art I can comprehend; I can even sympathize with it. But if this grave national question is to be decided by considerations of Chinese white

(CARVE turns to JANET as if for succour.)

JANET. (Calmly.) The doctor is just coming up.

CARVE. The doctor? What doctor?

JANET. A Dr. Horning. He says he's Dr. Pascoe's assistant and he attended Mr. Carve, and he wants to see you.

CARVE. But I don't want to see him.

JANET. You'll have to see a doctor.

CARVE. Why?

JANET. Because you're ill. So you may just as well see this one as another. They're all pretty much of a muchness.

(Enter PETER HORNING boisterously. A PAGE BOY opens the door but does not announce him.)

PETER. (Perceiving LOOE first.) Ah, Father! You here? How d'ye do? What did you think of my special on last Sunday's sermon? (Shakes hands with LOOE and bows to MISS LOOE as to an acquaintance.)

LOOE. Very good. Very good.

PETER. (Advancing to CARVE.) Mr. Shawn, I presume?

CARVE. (Glancing helplessly at JANET.) But this isn't the doctor?

PETER. (Volubly.) Admitted! Admitted! I'm only his brother, a journalist. I'm on the Courier and the Mercury and several other Worgan papers. One of our chaps failed to get into this room this morning, so I came along to try what I could do. You see what I've done.

JANET. Well, I never came across such a set of people in my life.

PETER. (Aside to LOOE.) Is he in service here, or what?

LOOE. Mr. Shawn was Mr. Carve's secretary and companion, not his valet.

PETER. (Puzzled, but accepting the situation.) Ah! So much the better. Now, Mr. Shawn, can you tell me authoritatively whether shortly before his death Mr. Carve was engaged to be married under romantic circumstances to a lady of high rank?

HONORIA. Indeed!

CARVE. Who told you that?

PETER. Then he was!

CARVE. I've nothing to say.

PETER. You won't tell me her name?

CARVE. I've nothing to say.

PETER. Secondly, I'm instructed to offer something considerable for your signature to an account of Ilam Carve's eccentric life on the Continent.

CARVE. Eccentric life on the Continent!

PETER. I shouldn't keep you half an hour, three quarters at most. A hundred pounds. Cash down, you know. Bank notes. All you have to do is to sign.

CARVE. (To Janet, exhausted, but disdainful.) I wouldn't mind signing an order for the fellow's execution.

PETER. A hundred and fifty!

CARVE. Or burning at the stake.

PETER. (To LOOE.) What does he say?

LOOE. Mr. Shawn is indisposed. We've just been discussing the question of the burial in the Abbey. I think I may say, if it interests you as an item of news, that Ilam Carve will not be buried in the Abbey.

PETER. (Lightly.) Oh yes he will, Father. There was a little doubt about it until we got particulars of his will this morning. But his will settled it.

LOOE. His will?

PETER. Yes. Didn't you know? No, you wouldn't. Well, his estate will come out at about a couple of hundred thousand, and he's left it practically all for an International Gallery of Modern Art in London. Very ingenious plan. None of your Chantrey Bequest business. Three pictures and one piece of sculpture are to be bought each year in London. Fixed price L400 each, large or small. Trustees are to be business men, bank directors. But they can't choose the works. The works are to be chosen by the students at South Kensington and the Academy Schools. Works by R.A.'s and A.R.A.'s are absolutely barred. Works by students themselves absolutely barred, too. Cute that, eh? That's the arrangement for England. Similar arrangement for France, Italy, and Germany. He gives the thing a start by making it a present of his own collection, stored somewhere in Paris. I don't mean his own paintings, he bars those. Unusually modest, eh?

HONORIA. How perfectly splendid! We shall have a real live gallery at last. Surely Anselm, after that

LOOE. Quite beside the point. I shall certainly oppose.

PETER. Oppose what?

LOOE. The burial in the Abbey. I shall advise Lady Leonard Alcar

PETER. No use, Father. Take my word. The governor's made up his mind. He's been fearfully keen on art lately. I don't know why. We were in front of everybody else with the news of Ilam Carve's death, and the governor's making a regular pet of him. He says it's quite time we buried an artist in Westminster Abbey, and he's given instructions to the whole team. Didn't you see the Mercury this morning? Anybody who opposes a national funeral for Ilam Carve will be up against the governor. Of course, I tell you that as a friend, confidentially.

LOOE. (Shaken.) Well, I shall see what Lady Leonard says.

CARVE. (Rising in an angry, scornful outburst.) You'd bury him in Westminster Abbey because he's a philanthropist, not because he's an artist. That's England all over.... Well, I'm hanged if I'll have it.

LOOE. But, my dear sir

CARVE. And I tell you another thing, he's not dead.

PETER. Not dead, what next?

CARVE. I am Ilam Carve.

HONORIA. (Soothingly.) Poor dear! He's not himself.

CARVE. That's just what I am. (Sinks back exhausted.)

PETER. (Aside to LOOE.) Is he mad, Father? Nothing but a clerk after all. And yet he takes a private room at the Grand Babylon, and then he refuses a hundred and fifty of the best and goes on like this. And now, blessed if he isn't Ilam Carve! (Laughs.)

LOOE. I really think we ought to leave.

HONORIA. (To JANET.) He's a little unhinged! But how charming he is.

JANET. (Prudently resenting HONORIA'S interest in CARVE.) Yes, he's a little unhinged. And who wouldn't be?

PETER. Got 'em, if you ask me! (Moving to leave.)

LOOE. (Moving to leave.) Honoria.

JANET. (Very soothingly and humouringly to CARVE.) So this is what you call being shy!

CARVE. (To JANET, who is now bending over him.) It must be stopped.

JANET. (As the others go out; humouring him.) Yes, yes! (Absently in reply to bows and adieux of LOOE, HONORIA, and PETER HORNING.) Good morning! (When they are gone, with a sigh of relief.) Well, it is a mighty queer place! My word, how cold your hands are! (Going quickly to telephone and speaking into telephone.) Please send up two hot-water bottles at once. Yes, hot-water bottles. Never heard of a hot-water bottle before?

[The Stage is darkened for a few moments to indicate the passage of time.]

## ACT II SCENE II

[TIME. Afternoon, four days later.]

[JANET is dozing in an easy-chair. Enter CARVE in his dressing-gown.]

JANET. (Starting up.) Mr. Shawn, what are you doing out of bed? After such a dose of flu as you've had!

CARVE. I'm doing nothing out of bed. (Twiddles his thumbs.)

JANET. But you've no right to be out of bed at all.

CARVE. I was afraid I hadn't. But I called and called, and there was no answer. So then I began to argue the point. Why not get up? I'd had a tremendous long sleep. I felt singularly powerful. And I thought you'd gone home.

JANET. Nay, that you never did!

CARVE. I did, honestly.

JANET. Do you mean to say you thought for a single moment I should go home and leave you like that?

CARVE. Yes. But of course I thought you might be coming back sooner or later.

JANET. Well I never!

CARVE. You've scarcely left me for three days and three nights, Mrs. Cannot, so far as I remember. Surely it was natural for me to suppose that you'd gone home to your own affairs.

JANET. (Sarcastically.) It didn't occur to you I might have dropped off to sleep?

CARVE. Now, don't be angry. I'm only convalescent.

JANET. Will you kindly march right back to bed this instant?

CARVE. No, I'm dashed if I do!

JANET. I beg pardon.

CARVE. I say, I'm dashed if I do! I won't stir until I've thanked you. I've been ill I don't know how many times; but this is the first time in my life I've ever enjoyed being ill. D'you know (with an ingenuous smile.) I'd really no idea what nursing was.

JANET. (Drily.) Hadn't you? Well, if you call that nursing, I don't. But it was the best I could do in this barracks, with the kitchen a mile and a half off, and a pack of men that can't understand English gaping at you all day in evening-dress. I dare say this is a very good hotel for reading newspapers in. But if you want anything that isn't on the menu, it's as bad as drawing money out of the post office savings bank. You should see me nurse in my own house.

CARVE. I should like to. Even in this barracks (imitating her.) you've quite altered my views of life.

JANET. Yes, and they wanted altering. When I think of you and that other poor fellow wandering about all alone on that Continent, without the slightest notion of what comfort is.... Well, I'll say this, it's a pleasure to nurse you. Now, will you go back to bed?

CARVE. I suppose coffee's on the menu?

JANET. Coffee?

CARVE. I think I should like some cafe au lait, and a roll.

JANET. (Rising.) You can have hot milk if you like.

CARVE. All right. And then when I've had it I'll go to bed.

JANET. (At telephone.) Are you there?

CARVE. (Picking up a sheet of paper from table.) Hello! What's this? Hotel bill-receipted?

JANET. I should think so indeed! They sent it up the second day. (Into telephone.) Hot milk, please, and let it be hot! (Hanging up telephone. To CARVE.) I expect they were afraid for their money.

CARVE. And you paid it?

JANET. I took the money out of your pockets and I just paid it. I never said a word. But if you hadn't been ill I should have said something. Of all the swindles, of all the barefaced swindles!... Do you see what it's costing you to live here a day?

CARVE. Oh, not much above four pounds, I hope.

JANET. (Speechless at first.) Any woman that knew her business could keep you for a month, a month, for less than you spend here in a day and better. And better! Look here: "Biscuits, 1s. 6d.!"

CARVE. Well?

JANET. Well (confidentially earnest.), will you believe me when I tell you there wasn't a pennyworth of biscuits on that plate? Do you think I don't know what biscuits are a pound?

CARVE. Really!

JANET. (Ironically.) "Cheapest in the end" but I should say the end's a long way off.

CARVE. (Who has picked up another paper, on mantelpiece.) What? "Admit Mr. Albert Shawn to Westminster Abbey, cloisters entrance.... Funeral.... Tuesday."... That's to-day, isn't it?

JANET. Yes.

CARVE. (Moved.) But you told me he wasn't going to be buried in Westminster Abbey.

JANET. I know.

CARVE. You told me Cyrus Carve had insisted on cremation.

JANET. (With vivacity.) And what did you expect me to tell you? I had to soothe you somehow; you were just about delirious. I was afraid if I told you the truth you'd be doing something silly, seeing the state you were in. Then it struck me a nice plain cremation at Woking was the very thing to keep you quiet.

CARVE. (Still more moved.) Then he's.... Westminster Abbey!

JANET. Yes, I should say all is over by this time. There were thousands of people for the lying-in-state, it seems.

CARVE. But it's awful. Absolutely awful.

JANET. Why is it awful?

CARVE. I told you, I explained the whole thing to you.

JANET. (Humouring, remonstrating.) Mr. Shawn, surely you've got rid of that idea! You aren't delirious now. You said you were convalescent, you know.

CARVE. There'll be a perfect Hades of a row. I must write to the Dean at once. I must

JANET. (Soothingly.) I shouldn't if I were you. Why not let things be? No one would believe that tale

CARVE. Do you believe it?

JANET. (Perfunctorily.) Oh yes.

CARVE. No, you don't. Honestly, do you now?

JANET. Wellm (Knock at door.) Come in. (Enter WAITER with hot milk.) Here's your hot milk.

WAITER. Miss Looe has called.

CARVE. I must see her.

JANET. But

CARVE. I must see her.

JANET. Oh, very well. (Exit WAITER.) She's telephoned each day to inquire how you were. She asked if you wanted a seat for the funeral. I told her you couldn't possibly go, but I was sure you'd like to be invited, whether it was the Abbey or not. Please don't forget your milk.

(Enter HONORIA LOOE in mourning, introduced by WAITER.)

HONORIA. (Coming in quickly, bowing to JANET and shaking hands with CARVE.) Good afternoon. Please don't rise. I've heard how ill you've been. I've only called because I simply had to.

CARVE. It's very kind of you.

HONORIA. Oh, Mr. Shawn, I know you didn't want him to be buried in the Abbey. I'm all for quiet funerals, too; but really this was an exceptional case, and I think if you'd seen it you'd have been glad they did decide on the Abbey. Oh, you've no idea how impressive it was! The Abbey is always so fine, isn't it? And it was crammed. You never saw such a multitude of distinguished people. I mean really distinguished, all in black, except, of course, the uniforms. Royalties, ambassadors, representatives from all the academies all over Europe. Rodin was there!! The whole of artistic London came. I don't mean only painters, but poets, novelists, sculptors, and musicians. The art students had a corner to themselves. And you should have seen the crowds outside. All traffic was stopped up as far as Trafalgar Square. I've had some difficulty in getting here. The sun was shining through the stained glass. And the music was magnificent. And then when the coffin was carried down the nave, well, there was only one wreath on the pall, just one, a white crown. All the other wreaths were piled near the screen, scores and scores of them, the effect was tremendous. I nearly cried. A lot of people did cry. (Genuinely moved.) There was that great genius lying there. He'd never done anything except put paint on canvas, and yet, and yet.... Well, it made you feel somehow that England does care for art after all.

CARVE. (After a pause.) And whom have we to thank for this beautiful national manifestation of sympathy with art?

HONORIA. How do you mean?

CARVE. (With an attempt at cold irony, but yet in a voice imperfectly controlled.) Did your brother relent and graciously permit Lady Leonard Alcar to encourage a national funeral? Or was it due solely to the influence of the newspapers written by people of refined culture like the man who gave his opinion the other day that I had got 'em? Or perhaps you yourself settled it with your esteemed uncle over a cup of tea?

HONORIA. Of course, Mr. Shawn, any one can see that you're artistic yourself, and artists are generally very sarcastic about the British public. I know I am.... Now, don't you paint?

CARVE. (Shrugging his shoulders.) I used to a little.

HONORIA. I was sure of it. Well, you can be as sarcastic as you like, but do you know what I was thinking during the service? I was thinking if only he could have seen it, if only Ilam Carve could have seen it, instead of lying cold in that coffin under that wreath, he'd (Hesitating.)

CARVE. (Interrupting her, in a different, resolved tone.) Miss Looe, I suppose you're on very confidential terms with your uncle.

HONORIA. Naturally. Why?

CARVE. Will you give him a message from me. He'll do perhaps better than anybody.

HONORIA. With pleasure.

CARVE. (Moved.) It is something important, very important indeed. In fact

(JANET goes into bedroom, but keeping near the doorway does not actually disappear.)

HONORIA. (Soothingly, and a little frightened.) Now, please, Mr. Shawn! Please don't frighten us as you did the other day. Please do try and keep calm!

CARVE. I (He suddenly stands up and then falls back again into chair.)

(JANET returns quickly to the room)

HONORIA. (Alarmed, to JANET.) I'm afraid he isn't quite well yet.

CARVE. No, I can't tell you. At least, not now. Thanks very much for calling. (Rises brusquely and walks towards the bedroom door.)

JANET. (To HONORIA.) He's not really strong enough to see visitors.

HONORIA. (Going to door and trying to be confidential.) What is it?

JANET. (With tranquillity.) Oh, influenza. Sometimes it takes 'em in the head and sometimes in the stomach. It's taken him in the head.

HONORIA. Charming man! I don't suppose there's the least likelihood of it, he's evidently very well off but if he should be wanting a situation similar to his last, I'm sure my uncle

JANET. (Positively and curtly.) I don't think so.

HONORIA. Of course you know him very well?

JANET. Well, it's like this. I'm his cousin. We aren't exactly engaged to be married

HONORIA. (In a changed tone.) Oh, I see! Good afternoon.

JANET. Good afternoon.

(Exit HONORIA.)

CARVE. (Who has hesitatingly wandered back towards centre; in a quite different tone now that he is alone again with JANET.) What's this about being engaged to be married?

JANET. (Smiling.) I was telling her we weren't engaged to be married. That's true, I suppose?

CARVE. But are we cousins?

JANET. Yes. I've got my reputation to think about. I don't want to coddle it, but there's no harm in just keeping an eye on it.

CARVE. I see. (Sits down.)

JANET. If nothing comes of all this

CARVE. All what?

JANET. All this illness and nursing and sitting up at nights, then I'm just your cousin, and no harm done.

CARVE. But do you mean to say you'd

JANET. (Stopping-him.) Not so fast! (Pause. She continues reflectively.) Do you know what struck me while her ladyship was telling you about all the grand doings at the funeral. What good has it ever done him to be celebrated and make a big splash in the world? Was he any happier for it? From all I can hear he was always trying to hide just as if the police were after him. He never had the slightest notion of comfort, and so you needn't tell me! And there's another thing, you needn't tell me he wasn't always worrying about some girl or other, because I know he was. A bachelor at his age never thinks about anything else; morning, noon, and night. It stands to reason and they can say what they like, I know. And now he's dead, probably because he'd no notion of looking after himself, and it's been in all the papers how wonderful he was, and florists' girls have very likely sat up half the night making wreaths, and Westminster Abbey was crowded out with fashionable folk and do you know what all those fashionable folk are thinking about just now - tea! And if it isn't tea, it's whisky and soda.

CARVE. But you mustn't forget that he was really very successful indeed.... Just look at the money he made, for instance.

JANET. Well, if sovereigns had been any use to him he'd never have left two hundred thousand of them behind him, him with no family. No, he was no better than a fool with money. Couldn't even spend it.

CARVE. He had the supreme satisfaction of doing what he enjoyed doing better than anybody else could do it.

JANET. And what was that?

CARVE. Painting.

JANET. (Casually.) Oh! and couldn't he have had that without running about all over Europe? He might just as well have been a commercial traveller. Take my word for it, Mr. Shawn, there's nothing like a comfortable home and a quiet life and the less you're in the newspapers the better.

CARVE. (Thoughtfully.) Do you know, a good deal of what you say applies to me.

JANET. And you now! As we're on the subject, before we go any further, you're a bachelor of forty-five, same as him. What have you been doing with yourself lately?

CARVE. Doing with myself?

JANET. Well, I think I ought to ask because when I was stealing (with a little nervous laugh) the money out of your pocket to pay that hotel bill, I came across a lady's photograph. I couldn't help coming across it. Seeing how things are, I think I ought to ask.

CARVE. Oh, that! It must be a photograph of the lady he was engaged to. He broke it off, you know. That was why we came to London in such a hurry.

JANET. Then it is true, what the newspaper reporter said? (CARVE nods.) One of the aristocracy (CARVE nods.) Who was she?

CARVE. Lady Alice Rowfant.

JANET. What was it doing in your pocket?

CARVE. I don't know. Everything got mixed up. Clothes, papers, everything.

JANET. Sure?

CARVE. Of course! Look here, do you suppose Lady Alice Rowfant is anything to me?

JANET. She isn't?

CARVE. No.

JANET. Honestly? (Looking at him closely.)

CARVE. Honestly.

JANET. (With obvious relief.) Well, that's all right then! Now will you drink this milk, please.

CARVE. I just wanted to tell you

JANET. Will you drink this milk? (Pours out a glassful for him.)

(CARVE addresses himself to the milk.)

(JANET begins to put on her things.)

CARVE. But I say, what are you doing?

JANET. I'm going home.

CARVE. What? Now?

JANET. At once.

CARVE. But you can't leave me like this. I'm very ill.

JANET. Oh no, you aren't. You're very much better. Anyone can see that. All you've got to do is to return to bed and stick to slops.

CARVE. And when shall you come back?

JANET. You might come down to see me one day at Putney.

CARVE. I shall be delighted to. But before that, won't you come here?

JANET. (After a pause.) I'll try and come the day after to-morrow.

CARVE. Why not to-morrow?

JANET. Well, a couple of days without me'll do you no harm. It's a mistake to be in a hurry when you've got all your life in front of you.

CARVE. (After a pause.) Listen, have some tea before you go.

JANET. No. (Holds out her hand, smiling.) Good afternoon. Now do go to bed.

CARVE. I haven't begun to thank you.

JANET. No, and I hope you won't begin.

CARVE. You're so sudden.

JANET. It's sudden or nothing.

CARVE. (Holding her hand.) I say, what can you see in me?

JANET. Well, if it comes to that, what can you see in me? (Withdrawing her hand.)

CARVE. I, I don't know what it is.... Something.... (Lightly.) I dunno! Everything!

JANET. That's too much. Good-bye! I'll come about this time the day after to-morrow.

CARVE. Supposing I have a relapse?

JANET. (At door.) You won't if you do as I tell you.

CARVE. But supposing I do?

JANET. Well, you can always telegraph, can't you?

(Exit.)

(CARVE, after finishing milk, suddenly gets up and searches on writing table: he then goes to the telephone.)

CARVE. (Into telephone.) Please send me up a telegraph form.

[CURTAIN.]

## ACT III SCENE I

[Parlour in Janet's house in Putney. A perfectly ordinary suburban interior of a small house; but comfortable. Table in centre. Door, R., up stage, leading to hall. Door, L., down stage, hading to kitchen and back premises.]

[TIME. Morning in early autumn. Rather more than two years have elapsed.]

[Discovered, CARVE reading newspaper at breakfast-table. JANET in an apron is hovering busily near him.]

JANET. (Putting cigarettes and matches down beside CARVE.) Want anything else, dear? (No answer from CARVE.) Because I must set about my morning's work. (CARVE continues to read.) Albert, are you sure you don't want anything else?

(As he still gives her no sign of attention, she snatches the paper away from him, and throws it on the floor.)

CARVE. (Not having moved his eyes.) The pattern of this jug is really not so bad.... Yes, my soul?

JANET. I've asked you I don't know how many times whether you want anything else, because I must set about my morning's work.

CARVE. Is there any more coffee?

JANET. Yes, plenty.

CARVE. Hot?

JANET. Yes.

CARVE. Then I don't want any. Got any bacon?

JANET. No, but I can cook a slice in a minute.

CARVE. (With an affectation of martyrdom.) Doesn't matter.

JANET. Oh yes, I will. (Moving away.)

CARVE. (Drawing her to him by her apron.) Can't you see he's teasing you?

JANET. She's got no time in the morning for being teased.

(She takes a cigarette, lights it and immediately puts it in his mouth.)

CARVE. And now you're going to leave me?

JANET. Sure you're all right? (He nods.) Quite sure you're happy?

CARVE. Jane

JANET. I wish you wouldn't call me Jane.

CARVE. But I will call you Jane. Jane, why do you ask me if I'm sure I'm happy? When a man has first-class food and first-class love, together with a genuine French bed, really waterproof boots, a constant supply of hot water in the bathroom, enough money to buy cigarettes and sixpenny editions, the freedom to do what he likes all day and every day, and, let me see, what else, a complete absence of domestic servants, then either that man is happy or he is a silly cuckoo!

JANET. You aren't getting tired

CARVE. My sweet child, what's the matter with you?

JANET. Nothing, nothing. Only to-day's the second anniversary of our wedding, and you've, you've said nothing about it.

CARVE. (After a shocked paused.) And I forgot it last year, didn't I? I shall be forgetting my dinner next.

JANET. Oh no, you won't!

CARVE. And yet all last week I was thinking about this most important day, and telling myself I must remember it.

JANET. Very easy to say that. But how can you prove it?

CARVE. Well, it does just happen that the proof is behind the sideboard.

JANET. A present?

CARVE. A present. It was all ready and waiting five days ago.

JANET. (Drawing a framed picture from behind the sideboard, and trying to hide her disappointment, but not quite succeeding.) Oh! A picture! Who is it? (Examines it with her nose close to it.)

CARVE. No, no. You can't take a picture like snuff! Get away from it. (He jumps up, snatches the picture from her, and exposes it on a chair at the other side of the room.) Now! (He sits down again.)

JANET. Yes, it doesn't look quite so queer like that. Those are my cooking sleeves, and that seems a bit like my kitchen, that's my best copper pan! Is the young woman meant to be me?

CARVE. Well, not to beat about the bush, yes.

JANET. I don't consider it very flattering.

CARVE. How many times have you told me you hate flattery?

JANET. (Running to him.) Now he's hurt. Oh, he's hurt. (Kissing him.) It's a beautiful picture, and the frame's lovely! And she's so glad he didn't forget.

CARVE. It is pretty good. In fact it's devilish good. It's one of the best things I ever did in my life. Old Carve would have got eight hundred for that like a shot.

JANET. (Sceptically.) Would he? It's wonderful how wonderful people are when they're dead.

CARVE. And now will she let him finish reading his paper?

JANET. (Handing him the paper, then putting her head close to his and looking at the paper.) What was it he was reading that made him so deaf he couldn't hear his wife when she spoke to him?

CARVE. This.

JANET. (Reading.) "Ilam Carve's princely bequest. The International Gallery of Art. Foundation stone laying. Eloquent speech by Lord Rosebery." Oh! So they've begun it at last?

CARVE. Yes, they've begun it at last.

JANET. Well, if you ask me, I should have thought he could have found something better to do with his money.

CARVE. As for example?

JANET. Well, I should have thought there were more than enough picture galleries as it is. Who wants 'em? Even when they're free, people won't go into them unless it's a wet day. I've never been in a free picture gallery yet that wasn't as empty as a church. Stands to reason! It isn't even a cinematograph. When I see rows of people in Trafalgar Square waiting to get into the National Gallery, then I shall begin to think it's about time we had some more galleries. If I'd been Ilam Carve

CARVE. Well, what should you have done, witch?

JANET. I should have left a bit more to you, for one thing.

CARVE. I don't want more. If he'd left me eight hundred a year instead of eighty, I shouldn't be any happier. That's just what I've learnt since I took lodgings in your delightful wigwam, Jane-, -money and fame have no connection whatever with happiness.

JANET. Money has, when you haven't got enough.

CARVE. But I have. You won't hear of me paying more than half the household expenses, and you say they're never more than thirty shillings a week. Half thirty, fifteen. Look at the balance it leaves me.

JANET. And supposing I had to ask you to pay more?

CARVE. (In a serious sympathetic tone, startled.) Anything wrong?

JANET. Well, there's nothing wrong, as it were, yet

CARVE. Jane, I do believe you've been hiding something from me.

JANET. (With difficulty pulls a letter from her pocket.) No

CARVE. I've felt it for several days.

JANET. You just haven't then. Because I only got it this morning. Here, you may as well read it. (Handing him the letter.) It's about the brewery.

CARVE. (Reading.) "Mrs. Albert Shawn. Sir or Madam." Why are shareholders never supposed to have any particular sex? "Sir or Madam. Cohoon's Brewery, Ltd., I am directed by the shareholders' provisional committee of investigation to request your attendance at an informal meeting of shareholders to be held in room 2009 Winchester House on Friday the 20th inst. at noon. If you cannot be present, will you kindly write stating whether or not you will be prepared to support the committee of investigation at the annual meeting. In view of the probability that the directors' report will be unfavourable, and the ordinary dividend either passed or much reduced, the committee wishes to be thoroughly prepared and armed. Believe me, Sir or Madam." Oh! So that's it, is it?

JANET. Yes. My father said to me before he died, "Keep the money in beer, Janet"; he said, "Beer'll never fail in this country." And there you are!

(She goes to fireplace, opens coal scuttle, takes out a piece of paper ready placed within, and sticks it on the handle so as to keep her hands from being soiled as she replenishes the fire.)

CARVE. (Lightly.) Oh, well! We must wait and see what happens.

JANET. Supposing the dividend doesn't happen?

CARVE. I never worry about money.

JANET. But we shall want to eat once or twice pretty nearly every day, I suppose?

CARVE. Personally, I am quite satisfied with a plain but perfect table.

JANET. You needn't tell me what you are satisfied with. You're satisfied with the very best at one shilling and sixpence a pound.

CARVE. I can place eighty pounds per annum at your absolute disposal. That alone will pay for over a thousand best cuts.

JANET. Yes, and what about your clothes and my clothes, and the rates and taxes, and bus-fares, and holidays, and your cigarettes, and doctor, and errand boys' Christmas-boxes, and gas, and coal, and repairs? Repairs! A hundred and eighty is more like what we want.

CARVE. And yet you have several times taken your Bible oath that my half-share of it all came to less than forty pounds.

JANET. Well, er, I was thinking of food. (She begins to collect the breakfast things.)

CARVE. Jane, you have been a deceitful thing. But never mind. I will draw a veil over this sinful past. Let us assume that beer goes all to pieces, and that you never get another cent out of Cohoon's. Well, as you need a hundred and eighty a year, I will give you a hundred and eighty a year.

JANET. And where shall you get the extra hundred?

CARVE. I shall earn it.

JANET. No, you don't. I won't have you taking any more situations.

CARVE. I shall earn it here.

JANET. How?

CARVE. Painting!

JANET. (Stopping her work and coming towards him, half-caressing and half-chiding.) I don't mind this painting business. Don't think I object to it in the least. There's a strong smell with it now and then, but it does keep you quiet in the attic while I'm cleaning the house, and that's something. And then going out making sketches you get exercise and fresh air. Being with Ilam Carve so long, I expect you picked up the habit as it were, and I'm sure I don't want you to drop it. I love to see you enjoying yourself. But you don't suppose people'll buy these things (pointing vaguely to picture on chair), do you? No; there's far too many amateur artists about for that!

CARVE. If I wanted, I could take a cab and sell that in Bond Street inside sixty minutes at my own price. Only I don't want.

JANET. Now, just listen to me. You remember that picture you did of Putney Bridge with the saloon entrance of the Reindeer Public House showing in the corner? It was one of the first you did here.

CARVE. Yes, I was looking for it the other day, and I couldn't find it.

JANET. I'm not surprised. Because it's sold.

CARVE. Sold? (Excited.) What in the name of

JANET. (Soothing him.) Now, now! Do you remember you said Ilam Carve would have got L1000 for a thing just like that?

CARVE. So he would. It was absolutely characteristic.

JANET. Well, I said to myself, "He seems mighty sure of himself. Supposing it's me that's wrong?" So one day I quietly took that picture round to Bostock's, the second-hand furniture man, you know, he was a friend of father's, and I asked him what he'd give me for it. He wouldn't take it at any price. Not at any price. Then I asked him if he'd keep it in his shop and sell it for me on commission. Well, it stuck in Bostock's shop, in his window and out of his window, for twelve months and more, and then one day the landlord of the Reindeer saw it and he bought it for six shillings, because his public-house was in it. He was half-drunk. Mr. Bostock charged me eighteen pence commission, and I bought you two neckties with the four and six, and I said nothing because I didn't want your feelings to be hurt. And that reminds me, last week but one they took the landlord of the Reindeer off to the lunatic asylum.... So, you see!

CARVE. (Serious, preoccupied.) And where's the picture now?

JANET. I shouldn't be surprised if it's in the private bar of the Reindeer.

CARVE. I must get hold of it.

JANET. Albert, you aren't vexed, are you?

CARVE. (Forcing himself to adopt a light tone.) How could I be vexed with two neckties to the good? But don't do it again, Jane. I shall go round to the Reindeer this morning and have a drink. If that picture ever found its way to a Bond Street expert's, the consequences might be awkward, devilish awkward. Because it's dated, you see.

JANET. No, I don't see. I shouldn't have said a word about it, only I wanted to save you from being disappointed later on.

CARVE. (In a new casual tone.) Just get me my cash-box, will you?

(JANET at once produces the cash-box from a drawer.)

JANET. And what now? I'm not broke yet, you great silly. (Laughs, but is rather intimidated by CARVE'S air.)

CARVE. (Having unlocked box and taken a bag from it.) You see that? (He showers gold out of it.) Well, count it!

JANET. Gracious! Ten, fifteen, eighteen, twenty? Two, four, twenty-six pounds. These your savings?

CARVE. That's what I've earned with painting, just at odd times.

JANET. Really? (CARVE nods.) You could knock me down with a feather!

CARVE. I'll tell you. You know the framemaker's next to Salmon and Gluckstein's. I buy my colours and canvases and things there. They cost money. I owed the chap two pounds once, and one morning, in the shop, when I was opening my box to put some new tubes in, he saw one of my pictures all wet. He offered of his own accord to take it for what I owed him. I wouldn't let him have it. But I was rather hard up, so I said I'd do him another instead, and I did him one in a different style and not half as good, and of course he liked it even better. Since then, I've done him quite a few. It isn't that I've needed the money; but it's a margin, and colours and frames, etc. come to a dickens of a lot in a year.

JANET. (Staggered.) And whatever does he do with them?

CARVE. With the pictures? Don't know. I've never seen one in his window. I haven't been selling him any lately.

JANET. Why?

CARVE. Oh, I didn't feel like it. And the things were getting too good. But, of course, I can start again any time.

JANET. (Still staggered.) Two pounds a piece? (CARVE nods.) Would he give you two pounds for that? (Pointing to portrait.)

CARVE. You bet he would.

JANET. Why! Two pounds would keep us for the best part of a week. How long does it take you to do one?

(Noise of motor car outside.)

CARVE. Oh, three or four hours. I work pretty quickly.

JANET. Well, it's like a fairy tale. Two pounds! I don't know whether I'm standing on my head or my heels!

(Violent ringing at front door bell.)

CARVE. There's one of your tradesmen.

JANET. It isn't. They know better than come to my front door. They know I won't have it.

(Exit, throwing off apron.)

(CARVE examines the portrait of his wife with evident pleasure.)

CARVE. (To himself.) That 'ud make 'em sit up in Bond Street. (Laughs grimly.)

(Voices off. Re-enter JANET, followed by EBAG carrying a picture.)

JANET. Well, it never rains but it pours. Here's a gentleman in a motor car wants to know if you've got any pictures for sale. (She calmly conceals her apron.)

EBAG. (With diplomatic caution and much deference.) Good-morning.

CARVE. (Whose entire demeanour has suddenly changed into hostility.) Good-morning.

EBAG. I've been buying some very delightful little things of yours from a man that calls himself a picture-dealer and frame-maker (ironically) in the High Street here. I persuaded him, not without difficulty, to give me your address. And I've ventured to call just to see if by chance you have anything for sale.

CARVE. By chance I haven't!

EBAG. Nothing at all?

CARVE. Not a square inch.

EBAG. (Catching sight of Janet's portrait.) Pardon me. May I look?

JANET. Oh, do!

EBAG. A brilliant likeness.

JANET. Who of?

EBAG. Why, madam, yourself? The attitude is extraordinarily expressive. And if I may say so (glancing at CARVE) the placing of the high lights, those white sleevelets, what d'you call them?

JANET. Why! Those are my cooking-sleeves!

EBAG. (Quietly.) Yes, well, it's genius, mere genius.

JANET. (Looking at picture afresh) It is rather pretty when you come to look at it.

EBAG. It is a masterpiece, madam. (To CARVE.) Then I may not make an offer for it?

CARVE. No.

JANET. Excuse me, Albert. Why shouldn't the gentleman make an offer for it?

EBAG. (Quickly seizing an opportunity) If you cared to consider, say, five hundred pounds.

JANET. Five hundred p -

EBAG. I came down quite prepared to spend and to pay cash. (Fingers his pocket-book.)

JANET. (Sitting down.) And if it isn't a rude question, do you generally go about with five hundred pounds in your pocket, as it were?

EBAG. (Raising his hands.) In my business, madam

CARVE. It's not for sale. (Turns it round.)

JANET. (Vivaciously.) Oh yes, it is. Somebody in this house must think about the future. (Cajolingly.) If this gentleman can show me five hundred pounds it's for sale. After all, it's my picture. And you can do me another one. I'd much sooner be done without the cooking-sleeves. (Entreating.) Albert!

CARVE. (Shy, nervous, and tongue-tied.) Well!

JANET. (Endearingly.) That's right! That's all right!

EBAG. (Putting down notes.) If you will kindly count these

JANET. (Taking the notes.) Nay, I'm too dizzy to count them. (As if giving up any attempt to realize the situation.) It fairly beats me! I never did understand this art business, and I never shall....(To EBAG.) Why are you so interested in my portrait? You've never seen me before.

EBAG. Madam, your portrait happens to be one of the very finest modern paintings I ever saw. (To CARVE.) I have a picture here as to which I should like to ask your opinion. (Exposing picture.) I bought it ten years ago.

CARVE. (After seeing picture.) Janet, would you mind leaving us a minute.

JANET. (Triumphant with her money.) Not a bit.

(Exit, L.)

EBAG. (Bowing to JANET. Then to CARVE.) It's signed "Ilam Carve." Should you say it's a genuine Carve?

CARVE. (More and more disturbed.) Yes.

EBAG. Where was it painted?

CARVE. Why do you ask me?

EBAG. (Quietly dramatic.) Because you painted it. (Pause. He approaches CARVE.) Master

CARVE. What's that?

EBAG. Master!

(Pause.)

CARVE. (Impulsively.) Look here! I never could stick being called "master"! It's worse even than "maitre." Have a cigarette? How did you find out who I was?

EBAG. (Pointing to Janet's portrait.) Isn't that proof enough?

CARVE. Yes, but you knew before you saw that.

EBAG. (After lighting-cigarette.) I did. I knew from the very first picture I bought from our friend the "picture-dealer and frame-maker" in the early part of last year.

CARVE. But I'd completely altered my style. I altered it on purpose.

EBAG. (Shaking his head.) My dear sir, there was once a well-known man who stood six feet ten inches high. He shaved off his beard and dyed his hair, and invented a very ingenious costume, and went to a Fancy Dress Ball as Tom Thumb. Strange to say, his disguise was penetrated immediately.

CARVE. Who are you?

EBAG. My name is Ebag, New Bond Street.

CARVE. What! You're my old dealer!

EBAG. And I'm delighted at last to make your acquaintance, sir. It wasn't until I'd bought several of those small canvases from the Putney man that I began to inquire closely into their origin. As a general rule it's a mistake for a dealer to be too curious. But my curiosity got the better of me. And when I found out that the pictures were being produced week by week, fresh, then I knew I was on the edge of some mystery.

CARVE. (Awkwardly.) The fact is, perhaps, I ought to explain.

EBAG. Pardon me. I ask nothing. It isn't my affair. I felt certain, solely from the evidence of what I was buying, that the great painter who was supposed to be buried in Westminster Abbey, and whose somewhat premature funeral I attended, must be alive and painting vigorously. I wanted the assurance from your lips. I have it. The rest does not concern me, at any rate, for the moment.

CARVE. I'll say this, you know a picture when you see it.

EBAG. (Proudly.) I am an expert, nothing else.

CARVE. All right! Well, I'll only ask you to persevere in your discretion. As you say, it isn't your affair. Thank goodness, I didn't put a date on any of these things. I won't sell any more. I'd take an oath never to paint again, only I know I should go and break it next week. I shall rely on this famous discretion of yours to say nothing, nothing whatever.

EBAG. I'm afraid it's too late.

CARVE. How too late?

EBAG. I'm afraid I shall have to ask you to state publicly that you are Ilam Carve, and that there must have been, er, some misapprehension, somewhere, over that funeral.

CARVE. (Aghast.) Publicly? Why?

EBAG. It's like this, I've been selling those pictures to Texel in New York. You remember, he's always been one of your principal collectors. He's getting old, and he's half-blind, but he still buys. Now, I rely on my judgment, and I guaranteed those pictures to be genuine Carves. Well, somebody over there must have had suspicions.

CARVE. What does that matter? There isn't a date on any of them.

EBAG. Just so. But in one of those pictures there's most distinctly a taxi-cab. It isn't a private motor car. It's a taxi.

CARVE. And if there is? No law against painting a taxi, I hope!

EBAG. (Again quietly dramatic.) No. But at the date of your funeral there wasn't a single taxi on the streets of London.

CARVE. The devil!

EBAG. Exactly. Texel is bringing an action against me for misrepresentation. I shall have to ask you to give evidence and say who you are.

CARVE. (Angrily.) But I won't give evidence! You've brought this on yourself. How much did you sell those little pictures for?

EBAG. Oh, an average of between four and five hundred.

CARVE. And what did you pay for them? I ask you, what did you pay for them?

EBAG. (Smoothly.) Four pounds a piece. The fact is, I did rather well out of them.

CARVE. Damned Jew!

EBAG. (Smoothly.) Damned, possibly. Jew, most decidedly. But in this particular instance I behaved just like a Christian. I paid a little less than I was asked, and sold for the highest I could get. I am perfectly innocent, and my reputation is at stake.

CARVE. I don't care.

EBAG. But I do. It's the reputation of the greatest expert in Europe. And I shall have to insist on you going into the witness-box.

CARVE. (Horrified.) Me in the witness-box! Me cross-examined! No. That's always been my nightmare!

EBAG. Nevertheless

CARVE. Please go. (Commandingly.) Please go.

(EBAG, intimidated by CARVE'S demeanour, picks up his pictures to depart.)

EBAG. (At door.) Your wife will perhaps be good enough to post me a receipt for that trifle. (Very respectfully.) Good-morning.

(Exit, R.)

(CARVE goes to door, L., and opens it. JANET is standing behind it.)

(Enter JANET.)

CARVE. You've been listening?

JANET. (Counting her banknotes.) Well, naturally! (Putting notes in her purse.)

CARVE. Here's a perfect Hades of a mess.

JANET. And it all comes of this painting. Art as it's called. (She finds her apron and puts it on.)

CARVE. (With an air of discovery.) Your faculty for keeping calm really is most singular.

JANET. Somebody has to keep calm.

(Voice off: "Butcher.")

CARVE. Anybody would say you didn't care a cent whether I'm Ilam Carve or whether I'm somebody else.

JANET. What does it matter to me who you are, so long as you're you? Men are so unpractical. You can be the Shah of Persia if you like, I don't mind.

CARVE. But aren't you convinced now?

(Voice off: "Butcher.")

JANET. (With an enigmatic smile at CARVE.) Coming! Coming!

(Exit.)

(The stage is darkened to indicate the passage of several months.)

**ACT III SCENE II**

[TIME. Before daylight on a morning in February. Fire burning in grate. Also a speck of gas. Otherwise it is dark.]

[CARVE is discovered reposing-in an easy-chair. Enter JANET with a candle.]

JANET. (Stiffly.) So you've not been to sleep either?

CARVE. (Stiffly.) Oh yes; had an excellent night in this chair.

JANET. (Going to fire.) Now, you're only boasting. If you've had such an excellent night (imitating him), who's kept up such an excellent fire?

CARVE. (Lamely.) Well, of course I looked after it now and then. I didn't want to perish in my solitude.

JANET. Then why didn't you come to bed, great baby?

CARVE. (Sitting up with solemnity.) Janet, we are a pair of great babies to have quarrelled like that, especially at bedtime.

JANET. (Simply.) Quarrelled?

CARVE. Well, didn't we?

JANET. I didn't. I agreed with everything you said.

CARVE. What did you agree with? I should like to know.

JANET. You said I didn't really believe after all that you are Ilam Carve, and I assured you in the most soothing manner that I did believe you are Ilam Carve!

CARVE. And do you call that agreeing with me? I know perfectly well from your tone that in spite of all my explanations and reiterations during the last three months you don't believe I'm Ilam Carve. You only say you do in order to soothe me. I hate being soothed. You're as convinced as ever that Ebag is a rascal, and that I've got a bee in my bonnet.

JANET. But what does it matter?

CARVE. (Cold and hard.) Well, I like that!

JANET. (Weeping.) It's not my fault if I don't believe you're Ilam Carve. I would if I could, but I can't! You're very cruel.

CARVE. (Jumping up and embracing her.) Hush, hush! There! (Cajolingly.) Who's being an infant now?

JANET. I don't pretend to understand this art.

CARVE. I hope you never will. One of the chief charms of existence in your wigwam, my child, is that I never hear any confounded chatter about art. Now, are we pals?

JANET. (Smiling reconciliation.) Darling, do turn the gas up.

CARVE. (Obeying, struck by her attire.) Why, what are you dressed like that for?

JANET. I was thinking of going away.

(Exit, L.)

(She re-enters immediately with kettle and puts it on fire.)

CARVE. Going away?

JANET. (Smiling.) Now do listen, darling. Let's go away. We can't stop here. This Ebag case is getting more and more on your nerves, and on mine too. I'm sure that's what's the matter with us. What it'll be next week when the trial comes on, I don't know, upon my soul I don't. It's all very well for you to refuse to see callers and never go out. But I can tell you one thing, we shall have those newspaper people on the roof in a day or two, and looking down the chimney to see how I lay the fire. Lawyers are nothing to them. Do you know, no you don't, because I didn't want you to be upset, last night's milk was brought by a journalist, with a camera. They're beginning to bribe the tradesmen. I tremble to think what will be in this morning's papers.

CARVE. (Trying to make light of it.) Oh, nothing will upset me now. But you might let me know at once if the editor of the Spectator calls round with the bread.

JANET. And I'll tell you another thing. That Mr. Horning, you know the breathless man on the Evening Courier that came to the Grand Babylon, he's taken lodgings opposite, arrived last night.

CARVE. Oh, for a machine gun, one simple little machine gun!

(Exit JANET, L.)

[She immediately returns with a tray containing bread, etc., and a toasting-fork.]

JANET. So I thought if we just vanished

CARVE. It's too late, I've had the subpoena. If I hooked it, everybody would say I was an adventurer.

JANET. We could come back for the trial.

CARVE. We should be followed.

JANET. Not if we start now.

CARVE. Now?

JANET. Yes, now! The back door. Before it gets light.

CARVE. Creep away in the dark! No! I'll go through with the thing.

JANET. Well, I shall travel alone, then. Here's my bunch of keys. I'll just explain to you where everything is. I daresay Mrs. Simpson will come in and clean up. She's not bad, as charwomen go.

CARVE. Jane!

JANET. Well!

CARVE. You're taking an unfair advantage of me.

JANET. (Putting tea leaves in teapot.) What if I am?

CARVE. You're only a woman after all.... And I'd thought so highly of you!

JANET. (Sweetly.) Then you'll come. Better brush yourself up first.

CARVE. What time is it?

JANET. (Looking at clock.) Seven o'clock.

CARVE. Where do you mean to drag me to?

JANET. Well, what about this Continent of yours that I've heard so much of?

CARVE. There's a train from Victoria at 8.30.

JANET. Very well then. We'll have another breakfast at Victoria.

CARVE. And the cab?

JANET. There isn't going to be any cab, nor luggage, rousing the whole street! (CARVE goes to window.) For goodness' sake don't draw those curtains, with the gas flaring up!

CARVE. Why not?

JANET. (Conspiratorial.) Supposing there's some journalist on the watch outside!

CARVE. I wanted to look at the weather.

JANET. Well, go to the front door, and mind you open it quietly.

(Exit CARVE, R.)

(JANET pours water on tea.)

(Exit, L.)

(Re-enter CARVE quickly.)

CARVE. I say, here's a curate pushed himself in at the front door!

(Re-enter JANET, L.)

JANET. No, he's come in at the back.

CARVE. But I tell you he's here!

(Enter JAMES SHAWN, L. Then enter JOHN SHAWN, R. Pause.)

JAMES. Now let me entreat everybody to remain perfectly calm.

JANET. Oh, don't worry about that. Nothing startles us now. A few curates more or less....

CARVE. (Sinking into chair.) I suppose this is the very newest journalism. Would you mind me asking a question?

JAMES. What is it?

(JANET makes the tea.)

CARVE. Why did you wait till the door was opened? Seems a pity to stand on ceremony. Why not have broken a window or so and climbed right in?

JAMES. John, is mother there?

JOHN. (At door, R.) Mother, how often shall I have to ask you to keep close to me?

(Enter MRS. SHAWN, R.)

MRS. S. I'm all of a tremble.

JOHN. (Firmly.) Come now, you mustn't give way. This is he (pointing to CARVE). Do you recognise him as our father? (JANET, who is cutting a slice of bread, stops and looks from one to the other.)

MRS. S. (To CARVE.) Albert, don't you know me? To think that next Tuesday it'll be six and twenty years since you walked out o' the house casual like and, and (Stops from emotion.)

CARVE. Go on. Go on.... To think that I was once shy!

JANET. (To MRS. SHAWN.) Here, you'd better come and sit a bit nearer the fire. (Very kindly.) Come along now!

MRS. S. (Obeying.) Thank you, m'm.

JANET. (To JOHN.) And which of you boys was it that had the idea of keeping a middle-aged woman perishing on a doorstep before daylight in February?

JOHN. How else could we

JAMES. (Interrupting him.) Excuse me, John.

JOHN. (Subsiding.) I beg your pardon, James.

JAMES. (To JANET.) All questions should be addressed to me. My brother John is here solely to take charge of our mother. We have done our best, by careful forethought, to ensure that this painful interview shall be as brief and as dignified as possible.

JANET. And couldn't you think of anything cleverer than to give your poor mother her death of cold for a start?

JAMES. How else could we have arranged it? I myself rang at your door for a quarter of an hour yesterday afternoon.

JANET. We never heard you.

JAMES. Strange!

JANET. No, it isn't. We took the bell off three days ago.

JAMES. I was told that it was impossible to effect an entrance in the ordinary way. Hence, we had to use craft. I argued that food must come into the house, and that it probably came in early.

JANET. Well, it's a good thing for you I happened to hear the cat mewing, or you might have had another couple of hours in my back yard. You're the eldest, I suppose.

JAMES. We are twins.

JANET. Really!

CARVE. As you say, really!

JAMES. I am the older, but the difference between us is not considerable.

JOHN. Now, mother, please don't cry.

JANET. (Having poured out a cup of tea, holds it before MRS. SHAWN.) Sugar? (MRS. SHAWN signifies an affirmative, JANET drops sugar into cup, which MRS. SHAWN takes.) You'll drink it easier if you lift your veil.

JAMES. Now, mother, you are sure you recognise this gentleman?

MRS. S. (Not very positively.) Yes, yes. It's a rare long while....

JAMES. He is your husband and our father?

MRS. S. (More positively.) Yes. And sorry I am to say it. (JANET eyes her carefully.)

JAMES. I think that suffices. (To JANET.) Madam, you are in a most unfortunate position. You supposed yourself to be a married woman, whereas you are nothing of the kind. I needn't say that as the victim of a heartless bigamist you have our deepest....

JANET. (Handing him a slice of bread on toasting-fork.) Just toast this for your mother, will you, and mind the bars. I'll get another cup or two. (Goes to sideboard and gets crockery.)

CARVE. And so these are my two sons! They show little emotion in beholding the author of their being for the first time. As for me, I hardly recognise them.

MRS. S. And is it likely, seeing they were born six months after you deserted me, Albert?

CARVE. I see. If it isn't indiscreet, am I a grandfather?

JAMES. (Toasting.) No, sir.

CARVE. I only wanted to know the worst. Silly joke about the fertility of curates, you've met with it, no doubt!

JAMES. Your tone is simply lamentable, sir.

JANET. (To JAMES.) Mind! You can do the other side. Now, take care; the fire's very hot. (In the same mild tone to MRS. SHAWN.) Twenty-six years, you say?

MRS. S. Yes. Albert was twenty-two then, weren't you, Albert?

CARVE. Undoubtedly.

JANET. And how did you come to find us out at last?

MRS. S. It was through an advertisement put in the paper by that Mr. Texel, him that's in this law case, offering a reward for information about a Mr. Albert Shawn who'd been valet to that artist man that died.

JANET. Oh! So Mr. Texel has been advertising, has he? (Giving a cup of tea to JOHN SHAWN.)

MRS. S. Yes, for anybody that knew Albert Shawn when he was young. "Albert Shawn," I says, "that's my husband's name." I'd been told he'd gone off in service with a painter or something of that kind. I married him as a valet.

JANET. (Pouring out tea.) A valet?

MRS. S. A valet, ma'am.... And the struggle I've had to bring up my children. (Whimpering.)

JAMES. Now, mother!

JANET. (Stopping JAMES.) That will do now! Give it me. (Taking toast and fork.) Here's some tea. Now don't pretend you've never seen a cup of tea before, you a curate!

(JAMES accepts tea.)

MRS. S. Yes, they would go into the church, both of them! I don't know how we've managed it, but managed it we have, surplices and all. And very happy they were, I'm sure. And now there's this dreadful scandal. Oh, Albert, you might at least have changed your name! I – I - (Partially breaks down.)

JOHN. Mother, I beg (MRS. SHAWN breaks down entirely.) Mother, I absolutely insist. You know you promised not to speak at all except in answer to questions.

JAMES. I think, mother, you really might try

JOHN. Leave her to me! Now, mother!

(Loud double knock off.)

JANET. (To JOHN SHAWN.) There's the post! Just go and bring me the letters in, will you? (JOHN hesitates?) You'll find them scattered about the floor in the hall. Don't miss any.

(Exit JOHN SHAWN, R.)

(MRS. SHAWN recovers.)

JAMES. And what do you propose to do, madam?

JANET. (Who has been soothing MRS. SHAWN.) Me? What about?

JAMES. About this, this bigamy.

JANET. Oh, nothing. What are you thinking of doing?

(Re-enter JOHN SHAWN with post, which CARVE takes and begins to read.)

JAMES. Well, I suppose you're aware that bigamy is a criminal offence?

JANET. There's a police-station in the Upper Richmond Road. Better call there. It'll be so nice for you two, when you're flourishing about in the pulpit, to think of your father in prison, won't it now?

JAMES. We, of course, should not prosecute. If you are prepared to go on living with this gentleman as though nothing had happened

JANET. Oh, I don't mind.

JAMES. Well, then, I doubt if we should interfere. But Mr. Texel's lawyers are already in communication with the police.

JANET. (Stiffly.) I see. (An awkward pause during which everybody except CARVE, who is reading his post, looks at everybody else.) Well, then, I think that's about all, isn't it? (A shorter pause.) Good-morning. (She bows to the curates, and shakes hands with MRS. SHAWN.) (To MRS. SHAWN.) Now do take care of yourself.

MRS. S. (Weakly.) Thank you.

JOHN. Good-morning. Mother, take my arm, please.

JAMES. Good-morning.

JANET. Albert, they're going.

CARVE. (Looking up absently and only half rising, perfunctorily and quickly) Good-morning. Good-morning. (Sits down.)

JANET. (To JAMES SHAWN, who is hovering near door L, uncertain of his way out.) This way, this time!

(Exeunt the SHAWNS followed by JANET.)

(CARVE rises and draws curtains of window apart)

(Re-enter JANET.)

JANET. (Cheerfully) Oh, it's quite light! (Turns out gas.)

CARVE. (Gazing at her.) Incomparable woman!

JANET. So it's true after all!

CARVE. What?

JANET. All that rigmarole about you being Ilam Carve?

CARVE. You're beginning to come round at last?

JANET. Well, I think they were quite honest people, those three. There's no doubt the poor creature once had a husband who did run off. And it seems fairly clear his name was Albert Shawn, and he went away as valet to an artist. But then, on the other hand, if there is one thing certain in this world, it is that you were never married before you married me. That I will swear to.

CARVE. And yet she identified me. She was positive.

JANET. Positive? That's just what she wasn't! And didn't you notice the queer way she looked at you as they went out? As much as to say, "I wonder now whether it is him after all?"

CARVE. Then you really think she could be mistaken on such a point?

JANET. Pooh! After twenty-six years. Besides, all men of forty-seven look more or less alike.... And so I'm the wife of Ilam Carve that's supposed to be buried in Westminster Abbey and royalty went to his funeral! We'll have some tea ourselves. I say, why did you do it? (Pours out tea.)

CARVE. (Casually.) I don't know. It was to save worry to begin with, and then it went on by itself and somehow I couldn't stop it.... I don't know!

JANET. (Endearingly.) Well, I've always told you frankly you've got a bee in your bonnet. (Drinking tea and turning over the post.) More letters from these newspaper people! What's this lovely crest on this envelope?

CARVE. It's from Lord Leonard Alcar. He says if we'll go up and see him to-morrow afternoon he'll be very much obliged indeed, and he may be able to be of assistance to us.

JANET. (Deeply impressed.) Lord Leonard Al ... Where's the letter? (Searches for it hurriedly. As she reads it.) Well I never! (Reading) "And Mrs. Shawn." I've got nothing to go in.

CARVE. Oh, I shan't go!

JANET. Why not?

CARVE. Well, what about this trip to the Continent?

JANET. Continent fiddlesticks. I've never been asked to go and see a Lord before....

CARVE. Now listen, Jane. What earthly good can it do? I shan't go.

JANET. I shall. So there! Six Dukes in the family! I wouldn't miss it for anything.

[CURTAIN.]

**ACT IV SCENE I**

[LORD LEONARD ALCAR'S study, Grosvenor Gardens. Door, back centre. Door, L. JANET'S portrait is conspicuous on a wall.]

[TIME. The next afternoon.]

[LORD LEONARD ALCAR and MR. TEXEL are coming into the room from door at back.]

ALCAR. You still go on collecting, Mr. Texel?

TEXEL. (Uncertain of his steps.) Well, yes. I've been amusing myself with pictures for pretty nigh forty years. Why should I deprive myself of this pleasure merely because my eyesight's gone?

ALCAR. Why, indeed! You have the true collecting spirit. Permit me (directs Texel's hand to chair).

TEXEL. Thanks, I'm on to it (Sitting down.) My sight's going steadily worse, but there are still a few things that I can make out pretty clearly, Lord Leonard. Motor omnibuses, cathedrals, English easy-chairs....

ALCAR. Well, I'm charmed to find you in such good spirits, and really I feel very grateful to you for accepting my invitation.

TEXEL. Delighted to make your acquaintance, sir. Two old collectors like us, rivals at Christie's. I wonder how many times I've cabled over instructions to my agent to smash you at any cost. Delighted to meet you, Lord Leonard.

ALCAR. We ought to have met earlier, Mr. Texel. Now I've got you here, I must tell you I've ventured to invite one or two, er, kindred spirits to meet you.

(Enter SERVANT.)

SERVANT. Mr. Ebag.

(Enter EBAG.)

(Exit SERVANT).

ALCAR. How d'you do, Ebag?

EBAG. My lord.

ALCAR. Let me introduce you to Mr. Texel. Mr. Texel, this is Mr. Ebag.

TEXEL. (Surprised, aside to LORD LEONARD ALCAR.) This one of your kindred spirits?

EBAG. (Also surprised?) Mr. Texel!

TEXEL. (Holding out his hand towards EBAG, who takes it.) Well, Mr. Ebag, I've made a special journey to Europe to get a verdict from an English court that you've done me up for about thirty thousand dollars, and if I get it I'll do my level best afterwards to see you safe into prison; but in the meantime I'm very glad to meet you. I feel sure you're one of the right sort, whatever you are.

EBAG. You flatter me, Mr. Texel. The gladness is mutual.

(Enter SERVANT.)

SERVANT. Mr. Cyrus Carve. Mr. and Mrs. X.

(Enter JANET. She hesitates in doorway. LORD LEONARD ALCAR goes to meet her.)

JANET. You Lord Alcar?

ALCAR. I am Lord Leonard Alcar?

JANET. My mistake! (They shake hands.) But why does this young man call me Mrs. X. I told him Carve, plain enough.

ALCAR. Did he? A slip, a slip! You've brought your husband?

JANET. Yes, but not so easily as all that. I'm afraid he's quarrelling out there with Mr. Cyrus Carve. They get across one another on the stairs.

ALCAR. Tut-tut. Excuse me one moment.

(Exit hurriedly.)

(Exit SERVANT.)

JANET. Mr. Ebag! So you're here too! Why, it's a family party.

EBAG. (Astounded.) How do you do, Mrs. Shawn? I beg pardon, Mrs. Carve.

JANET. It seems I'm Mrs. X now, didn't you hear?

EBAG. I expect the servant had received instructions. His lordship has a great reputation for wit, you know.

JANET. (Looking round.) And what's this room supposed to be?

EBAG. Oh, the study, probably.

JANET. Really! Not what you'd call 'homely,' is it? Rather like being on the stage.

(Enter LORD LEONARD ALCAR, leading CARVE on his right and CYRUS on his left. Servant closes door from without.)

ALCAR. Now we're all safely here, and I fancy there will be enough easy-chairs to go round. Mr. Texel, you already know Mr. Cyrus Carve, and you will be pleased to meet the talented artist who painted the pictures which you have been buying from Mr. Ebag. He has most kindly consented to be called Mr. X for the moment. This is Mrs. X, Mr. Texel.

(They bow, CYRUS shakes hands with TEXEL.)

EBAG. (To CYRUS.) How d'you do?

CYRUS. How d'you do?

CARVE. How d'you do?

ALCAR. (Observing that these three are already acquainted.) Good! Excellent! Now, Mrs., er, X, will you have this chair near the fire? (Fixes chair for her.)

TEXEL. (Indicating JANET, aside to EBAG.) Good looking?

EBAG. (Aside to TEXEL.) Very agreeable little thing!

TEXEL. Excellent! Excellent!

ALCAR. (Interrupting a gesture from CARVE.) You have all done me a signal favour by coming here. In thanking you, I wonder if I may ask another favour. May I?

TEXEL. Certainly. Among kindred spirits.

EBAG. Assuredly, my lord.

ALCAR. I would merely request you to control so far as possible any expression of your astonishment at meeting one another here. That is to say, any violent expression.

CARVE. (Gaily and carelessly.) Oh, very well! Very well!

(LORD LEONARD ALCAR waves the rest of the company into chairs, tactfully separating CYRUS and CARVE as much as possible. He remains standing himself.)

JANET. I suppose what you really want is to stop this funny trial from coming on.

ALCAR. (Slightly taken aback.) Mrs. X, I congratulate myself on your presence here. Yes, my ambition is to be peacemaker. Of course a peacemaker always runs the risk of a broken head, but I shall entrust my head to your good nature. As a proof that I really mean business, I need only point out that I haven't invited a single lawyer.

EBAG. (After slight pause.) This is exceedingly good of your lordship.

TEXEL. For myself I'm rather looking forward to next week. I've spared no expense to get up a first-class show. Half the papers in New York and Chicago are sending over special correspondents. I've even secured your champion humorous judge; and altogether I reckon this trial will be about the greatest judicial proposition the British public's seen in years. Still, I'm always ready to oblige, and I'll shake hands right now, on terms, my terms.

ALCAR. We are making progress.

TEXEL. But what I don't understand is, where you come in, Lord Leonard.

ALCAR. Where I come in?

TEXEL. Well, I don't want to be personal, but is this Hague Conference merely your hobby, or are you standing in with somebody?

ALCAR. I quite appreciate your delicacy. Let me assure you that, though it gives me the greatest pleasure to see you all, I have not selected you as the victims of a hobby. Nor have I anything whatever to gain by stopping the trial. The reverse. At the trial I should probably have a seat on the bench next to a delightful actress, and I should enjoy the case very much indeed. I have no doubt that even now the learned judge is strenuously preparing his inimitable flashes of humour, and that, like the rest of the world, I should allow myself to be convulsed by them. I like to think of four K.C.'s toiling hard for a miserable hundred guineas a day each. I like to think of the solicitors, good, honest fellows, striving their best to keep the costs as low as possible. I even like to think of the jury with their powerful intellects who, when we are dead and gone, Mr. Texel, will tell their grandchildren proudly how they decided the famous case of Texel v. Ebag. Above all, I like to think of the witnesses revelling in their cross-examination. Nobody will be more sorry than I to miss this grand spectacle of the greatest possible number of the greatest possible brains employed for the greatest possible length of time in settling a question that an average grocer's assistant could settle in five minutes. I am human. But, I have been approached, I have been flattered by the suggestion that I might persuade you two gentlemen to abandon the trial, and I may whisper to you that the abandonment of the trial would afford satisfaction in, er, influential quarters.

TEXEL. Then are we up against the British Government? Well, go ahead.

ALCAR. (Protesting with a very courteous air of extreme astonishment.) My dear Mr. Texel, how can I have been so clumsy as to convey such an idea? The Government? Not in the least, not in the least. On behalf of nobody whatever. (Confidentially.) I am merely in a position to inform you positively that an amicable settlement of the case would be viewed with satisfaction in influential quarters.

JANET. Well, I can tell you it would be viewed with satisfaction in a certain street in Putney. But influential quarters, what's it got to do with them?

ALCAR. I shall be quite frank with you. The dignity of Westminster Abbey is involved in this case, and nothing in all England is more sacred to us than Westminster Abbey. One has only to pronounce the word "the Abbey" to realize that. We know what a modern trial is; we know what the modern press is; and, unhappily, we know what the modern bench is. It is impossible to contemplate with equanimity the prospect of Westminster Abbey and its solemnities being given up to the tender mercy of the evening papers and a joking judge surrounded by millinery. Such an exhibition would be unseemly. It would soil our national existence. In a word, it would have a bad effect.

CARVE. (Meditatively, bland.) How English! (He gets up and walks unobtrusively about the room, examining the pictures.)

ALCAR. Undoubtedly. But this is England. It is perhaps a disadvantage that we are not in Russia nor in Prussia. But we must make the best of our miserable country. (In a new tone, showing the orator skilled in changes of voice.) Can't we discuss our little affair in a friendly way entirely without prejudice? We are together here, among gentlemen

JANET. I'm afraid you're forgetting me.

ALCAR. (Recovering himself.) Madam, I am convinced that none of us can be more gentlemanly than yourself.... Can we not find a way of settlement? (With luxurious enjoyment of the idea.) Imagine the fury of all those lawyers and journalists when they learn that we, er, if I may so express it, have done them in the eye!

TEXEL. If I wasn't going to come out on top, I could understand you worrying about your old Abbey. But I'm taking the part of your Abbey. When I win it wins, and I'm certain to win.

ALCAR. I do not doubt

EBAG. (With suave assurance.) But I do.

ALCAR. (Continuing.) I do not doubt your conviction, Mr. Texel. It merely proves that you have never seen a British Jury exercising itself upon a question relating to the fine arts. If you had you would not be certain, for you would know that twelve tradesmen so occupied are capable of accomplishing the most incredible marvels. Supposing you don't win, supposing Mr. Ebag wins

EBAG. As I assuredly shall.

ALCAR. Then we should have the whole world saying, "Well, they haven't given a national funeral to a really great artist for about a century, and when at last they do try they only succeed in burying a valet."

CARVE. (Looking round casually.) England all over!

ALCAR. The effect would be lamentable, utterly lamentable. You will realize that in influential quarters

TEXEL. But do you reckon this policy of hushing up things ever does any good?

ALCAR. My dear sir, it is the corner-stone of England's greatness. It is the policy that has made her what she is!

CARVE. (Looking round again.) True! What she is!

ALCAR. (Turning sharply to CARVE behind him.) Mr. X, your interest in my picture flatters me immensely

CARVE. (Interrupting him.) I see you've bought my latest portrait of my wife.

ALCAR. Yes.

JANET. (Starting up.) What's that? (She goes to inspect picture.)

CARVE. I suppose it would be abusing your hospitality to inquire how much you paid our excellent dealer for it?

ALCAR. Not in the least. But the fact is we haven't yet settled the price. The exact price is to depend on the result of our gathering.

JANET. Well, if anybody had told me I should find my own portrait, cooking-sleeves and all

(Inarticulate, she returns to her chair.)

ALCAR. And now that we have got so far, Mr. X, I should like to centralize the attention of this quite friendly gathering on yourself.

CARVE. (Approaching airily.) Really! (He sits.)

ALCAR. There are several questions we might discuss. For example, we might argue the artistic value of the pictures admittedly the work of Mr. X. That would probably occupy us for about ten years. Or we might ask ourselves how it happened that that exceedingly astute dealer, Mr. Ebag, came to sell as a genuine Ilam Carve, without offering any explanation, a picture which, on the face of it, was painted some time after that great painter had received a national funeral in Westminster Abbey.

EBAG. Sheer carelessness, my lord.

ALCAR. Or we might ask ourselves why a valet should try to pass himself off as a world-renowned artist. Or, on the other hand, why a world-renowned artist should pass himself off as a valet.

CARVE. Sheer carelessness, my lord.

ALCAR. But these details of psychology are beside the main point. And the main point is (to CARVE) Are you Ilam Carve or are you Albert Shawn? (To the others.) Surely with a little goodwill and unembarrassed by the assistance of experts, lawyers, and wigs generally, we can settle that! And once it is settled the need for a trial ceases. (CARVE assumes an elaborately uninterested air.) The main point does not seem to interest you, Mr. X.

CARVE. (Seeming to start.) I beg your pardon. No, not profoundly. Why should it?

ALCAR. Yet you claim

CARVE. Excuse me. I claim nothing except to be let alone. Certainly I do not ask to be accepted as Ilam Carve. I was leading a placid and agreeable existence in a place called Putney, an ideal existence with a pearl among women, when my tranquillity was disturbed and my life transformed into a perfect nightmare by a quarrel between a retail trades-man (indicating EBAG) and a wholesale ink-dealer (indicating TEXEL) about one of my pictures. It does not concern me. My role is and will be passive. If I am forced into the witness-box I shall answer questions to the worst of my ability, and I shall do no more. I am not cross. I am not sulking; but I consider that I have a grievance. If I am here, it is solely because my wife does what she likes with me.

TEXEL. Bravo! This is as good as the trial.

ALCAR. (Good-humouredly.) Will you answer questions here?

CARVE. (Good-humouredly.) It depends.

ALCAR. Do you assert that you are Ilam Carve?

CARVE. I assert nothing.

ALCAR. Are you Ilam Carve?

CARVE. Yes, but I don't want to be.

ALCAR. Might I inquire why you allowed your servant to be buried in your name?

CARVE. Well, he always did everything for me, a most useful man.... But I didn't 'allow' him to be buried in my name. On the contrary, I told various people that I was not dead but strange to say, nobody would believe me. My handsome, fascinating cousin here wouldn't even let me begin to tell him. Even my wife wouldn't believe me, so I gave it up.

(TEXEL does not conceal his enjoyment of the scene.)

CYRUS. (Grimly.) Which wife?

(CARVE twiddles his thumbs.)

ALCAR. But do you mean

TEXEL. May I interrupt, Lord Leonard? I could listen for hours to this absolutely stupendous gentleman. A circus is nothing to it. But aren't we jumping the track? I've got two witnesses. Mr. Cyrus Carve will swear that your Mr. X is not his cousin. And the original Mrs. Albert Shawn will swear that he is her husband. That's my case. How is my esteemed opponent going to answer it?

EBAG. In the first place, have you cross-examined this very original Mrs. Albert Shawn?

TEXEL. Come. You don't mean to argue that a woman could mistake another man for her own husband, even after twenty-five years or so?

EBAG. (Smiling apologetically for his freedom.) According to the divorce reports, they're constantly doing it after one year, to say nothing of twenty-five.

TEXEL. (Appreciative.) Good! That's good! Well, I may tell you right here that I had an interview with this gentleman's (indicating CARVE) ecclesiastical twins only yesterday afternoon, and they assure me that their mother is positive on the point.

JANET. (Meditatively.) Simpletons!

ALCAR. I beg pardon.

JANET. I daresay they preach very nicely, but out of the pulpit they don't what I should call shine, poor boys! Anybody could see she wasn't positive. Why, it wasn't until the old lady dropped in to have a cup of tea with us that I felt sure my husband's name really was Carve.

ALCAR. Then you hadn't credited his story before?

JANET. Well, it wanted some crediting, didn't it?

CYRUS. (With intention.) You only began to credit it after Mr. Ebag had called and paid you the sum of L500 in cash.

JANET. (After a slight pause, calmly.) Oh! So you know about that, do you?

CARVE. (To CYRUS, genially.) Cousin, if you continue in that strain I shall have to take you out on to the doormat and assault you.

EBAG. I should like to say

CYRUS. (Interrupting grimly.) Lord Leonard, isn't it time that this ceased?

TEXEL. (Heartily amused.) But why? I'm enjoying every minute of it.

ALCAR. I should be sorry to interfere with Mr. Texel's amusement, but I think the moment has now come for me to make a disclosure. When I was approached as to this affair I consulted Mr. Cyrus Carve first, he being the sole surviving relative of his cousin. That seemed to me to be the natural and proper course to adopt. Mr. Cyrus Carve gave me a very important piece of information, and it is solely on the strength of that information that I have invited you all to come here this afternoon. (He looks at CYRUS.)

CYRUS. (Clearing his throat, to EBAG and CARVE.) Of course, you'll argue that after thirty-five years absence it's a wise man that can recognize his own cousin. I'm absolutely convinced in my own mind that you (scorn-fully to CARVE) are not my cousin. But then, you'll tell me that men have been hung before now on the strength of sworn identification that proved afterwards to be mistaken. I admit it. I admit that in theory I may be wrong. (With increased grim sarcasm.) I admit that in theory the original Mrs. Shawn may be wrong. Everything's possible, especially with a bully of a K.C. cross-examining you, and a judge turning you into 'copy' for Punch. But I've got something up my sleeve that will settle the whole affair instantly, to the absolute satisfaction of both plaintiff and defendant.

CARVE. My dear fellow, why not have told us this exciting news earlier?

CYRUS. Why not? (Glowering at CARVE.) Because I wanted you to commit yourself completely beyond any withdrawing. I decided what sort of man you were the moment I first set eyes on you, and when I heard of this law case, I said to myself that I'd come forward as a witness, but I shouldn't give any evidence away in advance. I said to myself I'd show you up once and for all in full court. However, his lordship prevailed on me.

CARVE. Well?

CYRUS. When my cousin and I were boys I've seen him with his shirt off.

CARVE. True. And he's seen you with yours off.

CYRUS. Now just here (pointing to left front neck below collar), just below his collar, my cousin Ilam Carve had two moles close together, one was hairy and the other wasn't. My cousin was very proud of them.

CARVE. Oh!

CYRUS. (Ferociously sarcastic.) I suppose you'll say you've had them removed?

CARVE. (Casually.) No. Not precisely.

CYRUS. Can you show them?

CARVE. (Very casually.) Of course.

TEXEL. (Slapping his knee.) Great! Great!

CYRUS. (Staggered but obstinate.) Well, let's have a look at them.

ALCAR. (To JANET.) Then doubtless you are familiar with this double phenomenon, Mrs. X?

JANET. Yes. But he isn't so proud of his moles now as he used to be when he was a boy.

ALCAR. Now, gentlemen, you see how beautifully clear the situation is. By one simple act we shall arrive at a definite and final result, and we shall have avoided all the noise and scandal of a public trial. Mr. X, will you oblige us very much by taking your collar off?

JANET. (Jumping up.) Please, there's just one little thing. (To CARVE.) Wait a moment, dear. (To EBAG.) Mr. Ebag, how many of those pictures did you sell to Mr. Texel?

EBAG. Fifteen.

JANET. And you made a profit of over four hundred pounds on each?

TEXEL. (Boisterously, laughing to EBAG.) You did?

JANET. Fifteen times four hundred, that makes, how much does it make?

TEXEL. Six thousand, madam. Thirty thousand dollars. Great!

JANET. (To EBAG.) Don't you think we deserve some of that, as it were?

EBAG. Madam, I shall be delighted to pay you five thousand four hundred pounds. That will be equivalent to charging you a nominal commission of ten per cent.

JANET. Thank you.

CARVE. I won't touch a penny of their wretched money.

JANET. (Sweetly.) I wouldn't dream of asking you to, dearest. I shall touch it. Goodness knows what street we shall be in after this affair and with my brewery shares gone simply all to pieces! Now, dearest, you can take it off. (She resumes her seat.)

CARVE. (Lightly.) I'm hanged if I do!

ALCAR. But, my dear Mr. X!

CARVE. (Lightly.) I'm dashed if I take my collar off.

CYRUS. (Triumphant.) Ha! I knew it.

CARVE. Why should I offer my skin to the inspection of two individuals in whom I haven't the slightest interest? They've quarrelled about me, but is that a reason why I should undress myself? Let me say again, I've no desire whatever to prove that I am Ilam Carve.

ALCAR. But surely to oblige us immensely, Mr. X, you will consent to give just one extra performance of an operation which, in fact, you accomplish three hundred and sixty-five times every year without any disastrous results.

CARVE. I don't look at it like that. Already my fellow-citizens, expressing their conviction that I was a great artist, have buried me in Westminster Abbey, not because I was a great artist, but because I left a couple of hundred thousand pounds for a public object. And now my fellow-citizens, here assembled, want me to convince them that I am a great artist by taking my collar off. I won't do it. I simply will not do it. It's too English. If any person wishes to be convinced that I'm an artist and not a mountebank, let him look at my work (pointing vaguely to a picture), because that's all the proof that I mean to offer. If he is blind or shortsighted I regret it, but my neck isn't going to help him.

TEXEL. Brilliant! Then we shall have the trial after all.

CYRUS. Yes, but your brilliant friend will be on his way to South America before then.

JANET. (Sweetly to CYRUS.) I assure you it's quite true about those moles. That's why he wears those collars.

CYRUS. (Grimly.) No doubt.... (Repeating.) Nevertheless he'll be on his way to South America.

CARVE. (Gaily.) Or Timbuctoo.

CYRUS. (Significantly.) Unless you're stopped.

CARVE. And who's going to stop me? All the laws of this country added together can't make me take my collar off if I don't want to.

CYRUS. What about arresting you for bigamy? What about Holloway? I fancy at Holloway they have a short method with people who won't take their collars off.

CARVE. Well, that will only be another proof that the name of this island is England. It will be telegraphed to the Continent that in order to prove to herself that she possessed a great artist, England had to arrest him for bigamy and shove him into prison.... Characteristic! Characteristic!

ALCAR. (Who has moved across to JANET.) Mrs. X, can you

JANET. (Rising to CARVE, winningly.) Now, Ilam. You're only laying up trouble for yourself, and for me too. Do please think of the trial. You know how shy you are, and how you tremble at the mere thought of a witness-box.

CYRUS. I can believe it.

CARVE. (Smiling at JANET.) I've got past shyness. I think it was the visit of my fine stalwart sons yesterday that cured me of shyness. I doubt if I shall ever be shy any more.

JANET. (Appealingly.) Dearest, to please me!

CARVE. (Curt now for the first time, with a flash of resentment.) No.

JANET. (After a slight pause; hurt and startled; with absolute conviction, to LORD LEONARD ALCAR.) It's no use. He's made up his mind.

EBAG. I have an idea that I can persuade

JANET. (Hotly.) Excuse me. You can't.

EBAG. I have an idea I can. But (hesitates) the fact is, not in the presence of ladies.

JANET. Oh. If that's all (walks away in a huff.)

EBAG. (To JANET.) My deepest apologies.

(LORD LEONARD ALCAR shows JANET out)

TEXEL. Well, well! What now?

EBAG. (To CARVE.) You remember Lady Alice Rowfant?

CARVE. (Taken aback.) That doesn't concern you.

EBAG. (Ignoring this answer.) Pardon me if I speak plainly. You were once engaged to marry Lady Alice Rowfant. But a few days before your valet died you changed your mind and left her in the lurch in Spain. Lady Alice Rowfant is now in England. She has been served with a subpoena to give evidence at the trial. And if the trial comes on she will have to identify you and tell her story in court. (Pause.) Are you going to put her to this humiliation?

(CARVE walks about. Then he gives a gesture of surrender.)

CARVE. The artist is always beaten! (With an abrupt movement he pulls undone the bow of his necktie.)

(The stage is darkened to indicate the passage of a few minutes.)

## ACT IV SCENE II

(CARVE is attempting to re-tie his necktie. LORD LEONARD ALCAR is coming away from door back. JANET enters from door, L.)

JANET. (Under emotion, to CARVE.) Then you've done it! (CARVE ignores her.)

ALCAR. Yes, and I feel like a dentist.

JANET. You've sent them all away.

ALCAR. I thought you'd like me to. Mr. Ebag took charge of Mr. Texel. Your cousin Cyrus was extremely upset.

JANET. What did she say?

ALCAR. Who say?

JANET. Lady Alice Rowfant, of course. Oh! You needn't pretend! As soon as Mr. Ebag asked me to go out I knew he'd got her up his sleeve. (Weeps slightly.)

ALCAR. (Very sympathetically.) My dear young lady, what is the matter?

JANET. (Her utterance disturbed by sobs, indicating CARVE.) He'd do it for her, but he wouldn't do it for me!

ALCAR. I assure you, Lady Alice Rowfant has not been here.

JANET. Honest?

ALCAR. No. The mere mention of her name was sufficient.

JANET. That's even worse! (Rushing across to CARVE and pettishly seizing his necktie. CARVE submits.) Here! Let me do it, for goodness sake! Great clumsy! (Still tearful, to LORD LEONARD ALCAR as she ties the necktie.) Somehow I don't mind crying in front of you, because you're so nice and fatherly.

ALCAR. Well, if I'm so fatherly, may I venture on a little advice to you two? (To CARVE.) You said you didn't want to be Ilam Carve. Don't be Ilam Carve. Let Ilam Carve continue his theoretical repose in the Abbey and you continue to be somebody else. It will save a vast amount of trouble, and nobody will be a penny the worse. Leave England - unobtrusively. If you feel homesick, arrange to come back during a general election, and you will be absolutely unnoticed. You have money. If you need more, I can dispose of as many new pictures as you like to send.

JANET. I don't want him to paint any more pictures.

ALCAR. But he will.

JANET. I suppose he will. Why is it? As if we hadn't had enough bother already through this art business!

ALCAR. Yes. But artists are like that, you know.

JANET. (Affectionately reproachful to CARVE.) Child! Look how nicely I've tied it for you. (Shakes him.) Whatever are you dreaming about?

CARVE. (After glancing in mirror reflectively.) There's only one question. Last time they buried me in the Abbey, what will they do with me next time?

[CURTAIN.]

www.ingramcontent.com/pod-product-compliance
Lightning Source LLC
Chambersburg PA
CBHW071411040426
42444CB00009B/2204